Mystic throug Senses

A Book of Poems

BARNABAS TIBURTIUS

INDIA · SINGAPORE · MALAYSIA

Notion Press

Old No. 38, New No. 6
McNichols Road, Chetpet
Chennai - 600 031

First Published by Notion Press 2018
Copyright © Barnabas Tiburtius 2018
All Rights Reserved.

ISBN 978-1-64324-991-9

I dedicate this book of poems to my Parents who guided me to the love of knowledge; to Magi, my wife and companion, who gave me the love of life; and to my daughter Anne and my son in law, Graham and to my son Ignatius to my daughter in law, Caroline and my three grandchildren, through all whom I see the diversity of my inner self.

CONTENTS

ACKNOWLEDGMENTS

I would like to thank the many individuals who have been instrumental in the vast experience which has been the main source of inspiration for me in writing this book of poems. It would be impossible to name all but this does not mean that their inputs have been of any lesser value.

I specially wish to thank Janet Hutcheon and Graham Day, for being the perfect host in my travels in North and South Devon in England. They also provided most of the historical content on the topic of smuggling in the Devon coast. Janet was instrumental in organising a visit to Tintern Abbey and a cruise on the Dart. To Anne and Graham for the annual visit to different locations in England and Scotland which evoked creative emotions through their heritage or natural ambience.

I would like to acknowledge with gratitude the kind permission granted to me by Forward Poetry, UK for including some of the poems which I had contributed to their annual anthologies.

This book would not have been possible without the constant support of Magi, my wife.

I would also like to thank Notion Press for printing publishing and marketing this work.

INTRODUCTION

It is good practice to make one's intention clear as to why one has embarked on a project such as writing a book of poems. The literary world is replete with tomes of excellent verse and if one more is on the way, one needs to explain why the prospective reader has to take the task of perusing this work. For a change, this is one of those works that come from a person who has neither academically nor professionally taken to writing as a career. I had this innate desire to write poems from a very young age. Probably, what sparked that desire in me could be attributed to some very imperceptible experiences. This, I would like to share with you.

As a young boy, I had the good fortune of being gifted a collection of books by my maternal uncle. This collection contained Milton, Wordsworth and Essays of Carlyle. I romanticized, many a lazy Sunday afternoon, of writing like these great poets and authors. I started penning short plays and got the siblings to play the parts.

Love entered my life when I was doing my engineering graduation. As my fiancée and I were separated due to our studies, I used to write frequently to her. Most of my letters were accompanied by poems. I wrote a lovely eulogy for my grandfather, for whom I had great respect and admiration. I studied and trained to be a professional engineer, working thirty six years in the process control industry and visiting many cities in India and later in my career many places in America, Asia, Australia and Europe. These travels, that I was fortunate to undertake, and the wonderful experiences have fuelled the outpouring of thought in the form of verse. However, the profession and associated mental model that I developed did neither deter nor lessen my desire to write. I continue to write in the last sixteen years since I retired from my professional life and nature has been the main source inspiration both at home in my leisurely travels.

Heart of hearts, I was always and still am a romantic. I love beauty, appreciate the rich content of nature, the unpredictable emotions of humans and, above all, the magnitude and complexity of our cosmic existence.

The Japanese language has a word which is unique – it is Yūgen, and it is an important concept in traditional Japanese aesthetics. The exact translation of the word is very contextual. In the Chinese philosophical texts, the term was taken from, yūgen meaning "dim," "deep" or "mysterious." In the critical analysis of Japanese waka poetry, it was used to describe the subtle insightfulness of things that are only vaguely suggested by the poems. Why I highlight this emotional concept is that whenever I deploy my senses in a meditative deep observation, I sense the welling up of inner thoughts in verses. I have tried to capture these in these verses.

The internal struggle continued in my life between my love for literature, philosophy and science. Though I became an Engineer and towards the end of my active career, an international Management Professional, the love of rhyme and poetry remained etched in my psyche.

Science and Engineering gave me a comfortable living but poetry and philosophy gave me a wonderful companion and contentment in life.

Barnabas Tiburtius
Chennai
11 June 2018

A CHILD IS BORN

"The whole universe feels the presence and birth of a single child anywhere. So, what produces a child is not the father or the mother. It is the whole cosmos that produces the child.

Chandogya Upanishad

The Upanishads are a body of deep-seated knowledge. My quest for understanding the manifest had taken me many times into these writings that have been a veritable treasure trove of knowledge. My love of science and a constant urge to know more in the field of Philosophy and Cosmology has led me to believe that we are a perennial part of the manifest and the unmanifest entity. The inner self or the soul is permanent. The human body is the temporary vehicle. The soul changes the outer form or its residence many, many times in its journey through the universe until finally it rests in the Supreme Being.

In the cataclysmic origin my code was written

The holistic intellect of all that came into being

I was in the beginning in the scheme of things

Like an acorn, the nurturer of the mighty oak.

In the distant galaxies my existence was cast

The fallacy of time, existential perception twisted

Akin to the knurled and knotted creeper

Seeking light and moisture a survival act.

Through a thousand generation my being portrayed

The cosmic dust collating into meaningful mass

I was there hidden in the volcanic heat

And in the frozen stillness of the methane ocean.

Released by the tectonic and gravitational forces

Spewed out as inter galactic forces act

Squeezed through worm holes, carried on solar winds

I have travelled the unseen dimensions.

Vibrations mutate my being a million form

This new vehicle nature temporal provide

I have yet a billion visitations in the manifest

Before resting in a singularity, my true form.

CHASMS

I grew up in a large family, where the upbringing was very strict. Devotion and practice of religion was very ritualistic and exact. I remember the instructions I received as a young boy for my first communion and the picture of hell with Lucifer, which used to be prominently displayed during the instruction. Every act as a young man used to raise a lot of moral questions. The guilt consciousness used to be all-pervading. Fortunately, during my high school days, due to mild encouragement from my family friend and priest, I started reading many books on alternate schools of thought that existed in the Theological and Philosophical field and asked questions, which would be treated outright as heresy by standards that existed in those days. Though I would not say this was an explicit action, it sowed the seed of enquiry and an attitude to question the various inputs I received as a young man. I remember reading, during my school days, an imprimatur book titled "The Advent of Salvation" by Danielou. Though mildly reprimanded by the venerable priest who caught me in the act, he expounded the sanctity of church dictum and he explained to me that, as I grew in wisdom and age, I would be able to judge the values that are propounded in various writings.

I lie huddled in fear trembling sweat pouring,

Advent of the night my mind in a choking knot,

Twenty years of earthly life my conscience purring,

Always guilt in whatever done and subtly thought,

Catholic in my upbringing a constant reminder of hell,

The damnation and reward for every act performed,

My brain now etched deep chasms, a hollow shell,

Fearing every move chained, manacled and deformed.

I long for freedom an unchained existence a climb

Out of the chasm of fear I call to you oh! Brahma,

Knower of all, embodiment of rich knowledge,

A helping hand dragged from the depths of fear,

I may see the richness of wide-open world so full,

That during this transformation this quintessence,

For some destined purpose I may lead a life,

Without fear, challenging, imbibing knowledge,

Like a thirsty plant in the first monsoon rain.

This hungry mendicant's predicament, the satiating,

Gluttony bloating my senses, a benumbed feeling,

As I deeply digest, the initial hunger abated,

The beauty and power of thine supreme knowledge.

TRANSCENDENCE

Human beings are inherently seeking transcendence in their worldly existence. There is always a constant search for the meaning of our lives. All the pleasures of life do not give us the lasting happiness that we seek.

Every age has brought forth Mystics who were given that extra power to probe into the realm of the unknown dimensions, which we mortals are unable to fathom as we are trapped in this space-time existence.

We have a huge body of philosophical work on this subject. One teacher who motivated me a great deal is Sri Aurobindo. The following two sonnets are inspired by his writings.

Muted vibration reverberate the astral spirit,

Like a boulder awash in the midstream berth,

The waters glide a destiny far beyond writ,

In nature's sojourn, multitudes of force unearth.

Invoked through abated breath and still mind,

Sacred chants the resonance a metronome,

Measures the tide of life's energy to find,

A perfect harmony so not to cancerous groom,

Any malicious intent in a discordant mind,

To release from temporal bond the craving flesh,

This enriching ablution through the cosmic spring,

An existence transcending in purpose to mesh,

The divine will subtly implant in every being.

The sun-washed granite hills and whispering seas,

The shimmer of brooks in the sylvan wilderness,

A distant stellar array a perfect motion assays,

Ethereal support seeking harmony in seeming chaos,

Like a dance of a thousand sparkles in moonless sky,

Chorus of patterns one discerns varied as your thought,

Among this galactic brilliance many thriving earths lie,

Awaiting discovery in perpetual motion gravity brought.

If one thought we are unique in this existence sustained,

A form begot over billion years through miniscule change,

What of worlds, thru multitude abodes life maintained,

The twisted unfathomable forms we behold is but a range,

Universal energy construed to adapt to revealing science,

It is but the display of ever-present cosmic mind.

RANDOM WORDS

I had the fortune of meeting the great English author, Iris Murdoch, in Oxford and, as I wrote this short verse, her observation "Literature could be said to be a sort of disciplined technique for arousing certain emotions" came to my mind.

Many a time, I sit down with all the right intention to pen my thoughts or an article but suddenly, there appears a vacuum out of nowhere, which seems to suck out every little bit of the creative thought that was so much entrenched in my mind only a few moments ago. This phase of total absence of ideas seem to last forever but, as suddenly as it had appeared, this process of inactivity of the brain ceases and out pops a torrent of words and their proper sequencing that enables me to write a fine verse.

Random thoughts penned in disarray,

The state of my restless mind does portray,

Deliberate attempt dulls the incessant flow,

Featureless landscapes in my tired mind grow.

The torn sheets, the unkempt floor, strewn,

Casts rumpled shadows, as the misty moon,

Travels the firmament in tedious sequence,

mind fatigued; a tormenting hindrance.

Through sleepy eyes amidst the litter spread,

Casual words, a meaningful order is read,

Quickly captured on a fresh page of cellulose

A fine verse I can now lucidly compose.

INNER SANCTUM

Many times I wonder what lies deep down in the very heart of atoms. What if I had been given that special gift to travel to this inner space of Quarks and other fundamental particles? Can I find the divine imprint in this inner sanctum? When standing deep within a dense forest, there is only a semblance of sunlight that filters through to the undergrowth. May be I can get glimpse of hidden the sun as a fragmented sliver from time to time. This the nature of the splintered reality that we live in.

As long as we live in this space-time domain, it becomes difficult for us to have an appreciation of the reality in the macro or micro world. This poem is dedicated to this search.

The inner sanctum I cannot fathom,

I sought it in the glittering tabernacle,

Circumnavigating the holy of holies,

Yet I found an emptiness so oppressing.

I then went to the burning desert,

Perchance my ignorance to incinerate,

Like hooded monks, rosary in hand,

But perception gained a shimmering mirage.

I then searched the vast expanse of the universe,

A focus and knowledge wrought by erudite scholars,

I was lost in the immensity of my ignorance,

This state of utter incompetence calms me,

Realising in the emptiness of every emerging space,

That no name or knowledge can define, who thou art.

DIVINE ARTISAN

> In his thought-provoking book, 'Manifest Your Destiny'

Dr. Wayne Dyer writes:

"Ancient wisdom from the East reveals that the best way to know our future is to create it. Not from a separate God who lives apart from us in the heavens in an exterior realm, but his spirit, his force, his unconditional love lives within us, part of the same force we use in both our thoughts and words, which in turn, are our two creative forms of energy that we either knowingly or unknowingly use to create, manifest and determine our future destiny. Our entire life, conditions, relationships and outcome are unknowingly the product of our thinking, our creative forces within." Hence, seeking the ultimate reality outside ourselves is devoid of gratification that is permanent.

The universe in every cell of my body so resplendent

From microbes you shaped billions of years past,

An evolving design coaxed from forms reluctant,

A mutation to complex forms this expression cast.

Unlike the artisan shaping a vessel of clay,

You work from within, perennial energy the tool,

The substance and the architect; as you lay,

A cosmic plan in which there is a universal rule.

Like a spider casting an intricate silken web,

From its very bodily excrete a splendorous abode,

Withdraw every creation in waxing and waning ebb,

Into the self, a permanence of a consistent mode.

For this life so sublime, your artistry I've revered,

Then I thought with knowledge you have conferred,

This inward and cosmic journey reveals a fallacy,

I would then be worshipping myself in epic hypocrisy.

REFLECTION AND SERENITY

One morning not long ago, I had completed my morning meditation and took a basin of water and dipped my hand to wash my face. My face was reflected in the water due the angle of incidence of light coming in from the window. Then a thought came to my mind.

I was in a meadow where there was a clear pool of water from some hidden spring. This water had magical quality and the surface looked extremely polished. The stillness of the water is an attribute that I most admired.

Water is normally associated with purification, both external and internal. I was finding a new meaning of quick return to serenity and stillness. In our life, we always encounter turbulence but seek rest and peace.

Silver pool of liquid glass,

Framed with lush green grass,

Quality of reflection a separate class,

Inner truth and beauty transparent pass,

Stored in your depth this serene mass,

Quick sedimentation strips the polluting dross,

Your image clear in nature does surpass,

Those of silvered mirror or polished brass.

I genuflect in reverence upon your bank,

Stoop low, cupped my hands and drank,

This life-giving potion of superior rank,

Fed by a mysterious spring into this tank,

As the wavy image upon the crests clank,

My tormented mind this true reflection did yank,

A pattern to discern its implication deeply sank,

Into my subconscious mind, a stream of thoughts crank.

Thousand empty words and angry outbursts screech,

Dulls the mind with comforting speech,

Reasons well-appointed the conscience bleach,

Way of life rooted to the ego like a tropical leech.

Grant me the wisdom and state to reach,

Though your serene content my action breach,

Turbulence momentary, your ever-calm state preach,

A true reflection spiritual in nature you teach.

JOURNEY

During the many years of my business travels, I had visited various airports. Delayed departures used to be the order of the day in Indian airports due to the weather or the perennial technical problems that used to plague the aircraft. I remember once talking to a ground staff in Delhi airport. I got friendly with this man and over a cup of tea, seriously enquired what was ailing the aircraft as the announcement over the public address system had indicated a delay due to technical reasons. The man sheepishly replied that there was nothing wrong with the aircraft but the delay was due to a political VIP, who was somewhere in the great metropolis and intended to be on this particular flight.

Thanks to these delays, I have read every conceivable fiction. But, you cannot glue your thoughts on books when there are interesting events that are occurring around you.

I sat and watched the swarm,

The human mass shuttling between flights,

The air conditioner groaning, the air acrid and warm,

Stilled by my tired mind, my limbs fatigued muscles tight,

I ache for freedom, open space, green fields and fresh air.

By some unforeseen force the human mass is transformed,

Hive of activity as many flights announcements blare

What existence from the canned air of waiting halls,

To the conditioned and packaged atmosphere of the craft,

Jetting away to multitude of destinations,

My flight by some conditioned syndrome always delayed,

I wait, watch and study the floating individuals,

What one can learn in waiting halls in human nature,

Cannot be surpassed by what one can assimilate,

In the hallowed halls of universities and deep study,

Or in the best storehouses of knowledge.

A mother's tender farewell to the son departing,

A lover's caress and seemingly everlasting lingering look,

A child's confused emotion holding tight to the mother,

As the father says farewell on some long travel,

A group of evangelical minstrels clad in white,

Bibles clutched, Walkman and money belts,

Closed eyes, meditating on the holy word,

Or relaxing to the heavy metal beat of Judas Priest.

Then emerge this twosome oblivious to the world,

Caressing, kissing, hands intertwined, inseparable,

As though by some internal energy and affectionate force.

My journey announced by a melodious maiden,

I now arise with renewed vigour,

Having witnessed the affectionate wave that sweeps,

Transcending the multitude woes of this earthly travel,

I know that at this journey's end I will be united,

Despite the turbulence of this brief flight.

SOUL-STIRRING ART

Picasso and Dali always fascinated me. I do not claim to be an expert on modern art form. Perhaps, it is the mystery evoked by this art form that is the reason for this admiration. We live in a rather predictable spacetime with respect to spatial references. Rules have been enforced on the way two-dimensional and three dimensional geometry have to behave. It is when these rules are violated that one finds new interpretations that could possibly exist. Picasso's painting "Portrait of Dora Maar" and "Christus Hypercubus" by Salvadore Dali are classic examples of an attempt by these great artists to take man beyond the confirmed laws of dimensions. It is with this license one can interpret the modern art form from a deep-seated reference that is extremely varied.

Modern art also goes beyond dimension. This form of art can extract feelings and meaning based on one's life experience and the content of the subconscious mind. I chanced to come upon many paintings which might appear meaningless and especially one which was called "Feminine Force" and the flood of thoughts that came to my mind finds expression in the form of a poem.

I stood rooted, the deep colours stirring my soul,

Like a speedy stallion my thoughts race,

In this gallery of paintings, crayon and charcoal,

Deep thoughts crease my brow in this maze.

Intricate patterns with strong hues illustrate,

Dimensions hitherto hidden in this canvas,

Reveal a group of nobles this domain migrate,

Perhaps affairs of state, to mutely converse.

Wooden floor polished and varnished brown,

Matching the drape a damsel wears, a tartan,

Earthy colours, brings to the nobility a frown,

Attenuated tone, a firm hint of life Spartan.

The very fabric seems to split in a birth reverse,

Disgorging a mummified apparition face exposed,

The tapestry discontinuous a fragmented verse,

Agony portray in its lines, blatant isolation imposed.

Children play unfettered by guilt of remission,

An eerie spectre, a feathered companion in tow,

Floats in the chamber, a barricaded division,

Betwixt agony and the ecstasy terrestrial life bestow.

This parlour abundantly depicts life's way,

A splintered psyche, the many mental mould,

That our every human act and relation hold sway,

Transcend the bestial veneer to joy untold.

THE ARCH

Some memories always lurk in your mind based on a subconscious trigger in response to one's feeling at a specific moment in life. I was assigned a big responsibility in Asia Pacific and had taken up residence in Singapore. My wife was with me and the children were all grown up with their own lives. One day, on returning from the office, I was suddenly overcome by a feeling of total loss of purpose. Many things flashed across my tired mind and I wondered how wonderful it would be if I can be away in some remote location, probably a spot off the beaten track, just me and nature in all its glory. This thought was very brief. After a very short time, I was back in front of my Laptop looking at my mail and planning for the next day. Months later, when I sat down to write, the fleeting thought returned and gave me the inspiration to pen this poem.

Alighting from his car at the end of a workday long,

Heard his joints creak, muscles ache, teeth clang,

Dragging his frame he pondered what is wrong,

His clueless mind searched as to where he belong.

The portal to his home he proudly designed,

Now appeared a barricade of steel and chrome

Every step his last drop of energy consigned,

Trapped in his ambitions, an airless astrodome.

He slumped on the soft cushions that his limbs caressed,

Flung the crafted case, as if to quickly rid of an appendage,

That grew through some mutation his body ingressed,

Lost in thought wondering ways to end this bondage.

Like some automaton his hands move to wrap the remote,

Rummaging the channels, the flashing images deftly burn,

A kaleidoscope of pictures galloping with ungainly trot,

The sweet song of birds arrests the searching sojourn.

Nature the soothing medication of the weary mind,

Calls to his senses a snatched momentary retreat,

Among the flora, a melody wafting in the wind,

some scintillating vibration, a winged angel's feat.

The comforts and money is no comparable match,

To the tranquillity of nature, man's very essence,

Victor am I in my conquests, no moments of joy to snatch

I will to nature return to renew my spiritual lessons.

Packing a bag without a care, a destination nature find,

His Jaguar devouring miles, a path of grime and silt,

A rustic beaten track, a road less travelled unwind,

Through the hills to a crafted arch eon built.

A great lesson you teach in this nature preserve,

Lofty goals and enduring vision need patience and toil

A symbiotic relationship constant energy conserve,

Every creation has purpose and a place in this soil.

HOLDING HANDS

I wrote this poem for the Diamond wedding Jubilee of my parents. My parents are a great example of faith in the Almighty. The mutual support that they have provided to each other is an example of true partnership. This poem is a tribute to the divine hand that guides us all in this life.

Three score years have elapsed since I held your hand,

Ever present trials have not any measure weakened,

The firm grip or, soft touch or a gentle command,

To find my own path with courage to the very end.

Guiding steps and words of outpouring wisdom,

A gentle nudge to open my tiring eye,

This tortuous path traverse, as the righteous of Sodom,

I was many a time spared the earthly holocaust many die.

In moments, I perennially long for your touch assuring,

Many chores the body eroded, your bond grows strong,

The faltering steps, I do not care, for subtly fostering,

In your strength, I travel the distance my effort strong.

Deep gratitude wells in my heart for the path shown,

For all the precious gifts whether of joy or sorrow,

A prayer I send to the seeds far and wide I have sown,

To live in the strength, your divine hands bestow.

FROM A CHOSEN ONE

> "Death is certain for all that is born and birth for that dies. Therefore for what is unavoidable You should not be distressed."
>
> Bhagavad Gita Chapter II: 27

I wrote this poem as a final farewell to my friend, who was the Chairman of the company we helped establish in India. Ian Hutcheon was a visionary, who was capable of seeing through the murky mist of human failings. He was a great humanist and believed in the value of dedication. He was like a Banyan tree, rooted in many cultures, with great understanding of people with whom he came in contact.

You had that intellectual fire in your eye sparkling,

The very first day you came to my city calling,

I saw a visionary, inquisitive in knowledge collating,

Open to one and all, no culture or belief intervening.

Your chosen few like the disciples of yore,

Travelled the globe your innovative spirit to spread,

Every continent sings your name in safety folklore,

Unique technology in a million device you've in-bred.

You are the germinator of this structured world,

An edifice of epic dimension built to your design,

In its foundation lie the solid strata of values untold,

Fortify this bedrock through your spirit consign.

I came from the east that you so deeply loved,

The many evening of Veda, Gnostic or Lao Tzu,

I was the doubting Thomas, the disciple beloved,

Wondering what reincarnation could be you?

Transparency and truth your virtue and form,

No malice in your act or ever streaming thought,

Thank you for the trust, an onerous task to perform,

A prayer I invoke at this separation so distraught.

May your spirit reside in the seeker's need,

Of untarnished knowledge in this world so void,

Human values, I upon thine passing intercede,

Be resurrected in every entrepreneurial effort deployed.

I SPEAK FOR YOU MY FRIEND

I lost my sister-in-law to brain tumour when she was very young. She had a high degree of respect for my knowledge and always enjoyed sharing her thoughts on various subjects. I wrote this poem as a tribute to this great soul.

To you the trinity, creator, preserver and Transformer,

I dedicated my manifestation, unlike the pointed apex,

Of a triangle, you are the eternal, resplendent reformer,

The cosmic mind, three segments beyond the vortex.

You churned my essence two score and more year,

A time eternal in your domain ever concurrent flowing,

I know you weaned me away from those to my heart dear,

A need to serve in your divine plan like a petal unfolding.

Linger to comfort in memory and resplendent thought,

Wipe away the tears that flow and lighten heart's burden,

I am near you, but unmanifest, this transition wrought,

The undying soul freed from the bonds of earthly tendon.

A Journey of seeking order within the seeming chaos,

In myriad divine creation seeking truth concealed,

You have chosen and speeded my spirit to the cosmos,

Higher dimension, superior consciousness is revealed.

I loved the flowers in your garden, the two, my reflection,

A prayer in my essence for the comfort propagation,

To the new order of my form I surrender in genuflection,

Grieve not for life in true nature has no termination.

The cosmic wheel spins towards a true convergence,

Drawn to cataclysmic extremities of existential presence,

Every creation imperceptible in their transcendence,

As I now await our grand unification in divine essence.

REMEMBERING WITH GRATITUDE

Many people touch your life. One such person was my father's younger brother. He was responsible for my joining the seminary, where I learned Latin and a disciplined way of life. His life was spent as a dedicated priest serving the poor and leprosy afflicted people while my life took a different path. This is a dedication I wrote on his completing the golden jubilee of his service to humanity.

Holding your hand, I stepped out a child little speaking,

Your comforting words I recall as we took the long path,

A journey of immense proportion, divine grace seeking,

Steadfast, undeterred by poor health or Latin's wrath.

Piety your weapon in spiritual strength a slow evolution,

Lightly borne the many chores thrust upon your shoulder,

The printed media and graphic arts gained your devotion,

Gratitude rests on many a heart, to you their life moulder.

Testimony to your untainted devotion and life dedication,

A disciple you became at the very seat of church power,

The Roman citadel where Peter in glorious vindication,

His life sacrifice for many nations to Christ empower.

You came, a song in your heart and a prayer on your lips,

Your native soil is blessed with your benevolence,

You nurture with care, what society from its fold rips,

This task bears a stamp of divine procreative resemblance.

The child that you led at your first evangelizing mission,

Now stands tall and happy in knowledge gained,

But forever dedicated to darkness dispel for better vision,

Appreciation in invocation rests till life breath drained.

We set out together on a tortuous path five decades past,

Different paths to seek man's status a divine culmination,

Through God's omnipotent wisdom to each a mantle cast,

In gratitude remember that first step in divine ordination.

UNEASY LIES THE HEAD

In my career, from the very first job as construction engineer till my tenure in Asia Pacific, I have seen thousands of workers who are engaged in back-breaking manual labour day after day for a meagre reward. The poem is a dedication to these karma yogis.

I rest my head oblique for want of a pillow,

The hardened cot, generations of use and abuse,

My weary frame cast in this universal mould,

A respite attempted by force of tired limbs,

The heavy summer air hangs like a blanket,

A heady mix of moisture and woody smoke,

The remnants of a frugal meal cooked wafting,

Insatiate hunger and insect hums a concoction,

A virulent catalyst for this insomniac state,

No slumber to induce a pleasurable dream,

Medication for the woes for this crushing pain,

Tossing and turning I lay awake.

Creeping fingers of dawn claw upon the firmament,

Cattle restless strain on their tether for release,

The meadows of lush grass, waiting, weep with dew,

A tasty amalgamation of food and divine drink

Ere the sun climbs the cloudless azure sky,

My brow is beaded with glistening sweat,

Another long day of relentless toil,

Some small reward is all that I seek.

SAINTLY SISTER

This is a tribute to a saintly Nun, who works tirelessly despite her own poor health, for the benefit of all children who are under her care.

I look to your countenance radiating peace,

Many toils deeply etched, thoughts imprint,

Silent prayers in coded lines forehead crease,

A ready smile glowing from within, radiant glint,

Sparkles in those eyes priceless masterpiece,

Mirroring spirituality and a caring human tint.

I envy the thousand children in your care,

Perennial bestowed thine bounty and reach,

Suckling the sweet nectar of the divine fare,

Inculcating the infecting spirit no sermon preach,

You are a source of joy an enigmatic flare,

Scorching with cleansing heat, spiritual bleach.

I long for the quietude and serenity you portray,

Thus I look upon the mirror mine eyes rummage,

In your direction to fathom some elucidation convey,

Perhaps in this moment juxtaposition of image,

You may the hidden anchors involuntarily betray,

Pardon this dissection no affront to your personage.

This prayer I always have in my tormented heart,

Much given, I agonise over the inadequate content,

May you be bestowed the force of a high-strung dart,

For the archer knows the choice and the intent,

He has set you free upon this terrain to play the part,

I look to you, a meaning to discern from life well spent.

CRAFTED HANDS

In India, where I live, the decoration of the bride's hand and feet with henna is a common practice. The elaborate pattern, the silk-brocaded sari and jewellery speak volumes of the tradition of an Indian wedding... a practice that is also common in the Middle East. I have been to many weddings and seen the lovely hands of the bride decorated with beautiful intricate patterns. This image evoked many thoughts.

I had just completed reading a very good fiction, "Mirage" by Shoheir Kashoggi. The treatment meted out to women in some societies could be bordering on torture. This has been well illustrated in Kashoggi's book. The fallacy of the moment, where a bride is all decked up, struck a chord in me... the brief moment of joy and happiness compared to the eternity of suffering in marital life. I dedicate this poem to those silently suffering ignominy in a thousand homes.

A hundred melodious voices sing and swirl,

Joyous occasion a union boisterously to celebrate,

Rustle of sequined garment sweep in a twirl,

Little beads glide in rhythmic chime upon the carpet.

Age dissolves in vibrant spirit, a brief window of time,

When the female fortitude is let loose on this floor,

To lift your voice and proclaim freedom sublime,

Pent up emotions since womanhood advent stored.

Sweet smell of perfume pervades the decorated hall,

Young bodies fresh from the aromatic purifying bath,

Pour forth the contagious energy and enthral,

In each other's company, no fear of elder's wrath.

Henna girls grind and test the paste herbal,

A viscous mix that the deft strokes will extrude,

Intricate patterns, the very symbol non-verbal,

Complex existence, this young bride's life will intrude.

Freedom is no birth right but gender defined,

This kingdom of wealth bejewels the crafted hands,

Yet this artistry wanes a lifecycle in nature destined,

So too are short-lived female liberty in these lands.

MONSOON

An eagerly-awaited annual event that occurs in India is the onset of the monsoon. The build-up can be wrought with anxiety as the months of torrid heat that precede the monsoon can sap your energy in droves and you start longing for the cool caress of the rain on your face. It was on one of those sultry afternoons in the month of May that I wrote this poem.

Dark clouds hang on the horizon low,

Waiting as though for some coded sign.

To unburden a toil, the locked up pressure blow,

The parched soil screaming for life-giving rain,

A weary labourer ploughs burrows deep,

In the hope that trenches will plenty hold,

Enough sustenance, the seed, the water and reap,

A harvest to live and lessen perennial misery untold.

The cowherd slumbers under the lone tree,

Cattle, listless in the pre-monsoon oppressive heat,

Wander dislodging the fly and nagging flee,

Searching for fodder an undiscovered shrub a treat,

The farmer looks imploring to the relentless sun,

Beseeching a rapid travel in the firmament to send,

Cooler eve, the pouring sweat ceasing, day's task done,

A rest in the hope that on the morrow rain will descend.

The dawn is silent the cock don't crow,

An ominous premonition, death foretold for the seed,

Fond hopes harboured like a prisoner in death row,

Ebbs away as the sun blazes oblivious to human need

Seeds clinging to subterranean moisture for nourishment,

Supplications, million drops of sweat and human tears,

Now tentatively probes for elements life's basic rudiment,

Bold in hope uncaring and undaunted by future fears.

Shyly like the newly wed bride lifting the veil,

A single green leaf breaks forth from the earthy tomb,

Seeking life from above heedless of dangers and travail,

New existence drawing life from the withering womb,

Imploring now with genuflection in the westerly wind,

The great motive forces of nature the heat and the cold,

To churn the moisture and maintain a steady grind

The heat pump to relieve the human misery untold.

BATHING IN THE BROOK

I had gone to visit my sister-in-law in the town of Tiruchirappalli. This is the famous historical town where Sir Robert Clive made residence. Away from the bustle of the town, within two hours of leisurely drive, lie the foothills of the mountain range that stretches up to Yercaud, the hill station near Salem. It had been three hot days in the town and suggestion was made to go to the little brook that cascades down the hill and take an early morning dip. After a backbreaking ride in an old van we arrived at the destination. What was in store for the tired limbs and parched soul is penned as a verse.

A cool breeze from the foothills waft,

This early morn ere the sun rays kiss,

The dew drenched herbs and glistening shaft,

Birds brightly vested sing in enchanted bliss,

Amidst the rustle and the blush of the wood,

I hear the gentle tumbling of a virgin stream,

A roaring act follows this subtle prelude,

A cataract, where a million drops scream.

Through the centuries a gallery of stone,

Well-polished some rotund to perfection,

The terrain awash lay bare to the bone,

An eerie landscape nature's true reflection.

The thorny bush on the serrated banks,

Have caught a bounty of drifting relic,

Some talisman or medallion signifying rank,

Or a holy thread denuded from a bathing cleric.

I sit on a large boulder cross-legged,

Meditating on the perennial source of life,

When a chameleon of rare beauty pegged,

A darting cricket and quickly ends its strife.

Pleading eyes set in a green pointed head,

Begs for understanding, the nourishing need,

I stare mesmerized as she gaily fled,

Vanishing against the stalk of a swaying reed.

As the salubrious milieu wraps my soul,

I hear the laughter of the frolicking current,

Drenched in the cool waters, glances deftly stole,

A free spirit stirring the seething torrent.

Lissom lass thin veil over her bosom,

Child of the river merging with the terrain,

I wonder if she were the river's ransom,

To draw me to its heart forever remain.

STORM BREWING

I live in Chennai. This is the monsoon season and the east coast of India experiences a few cyclones during this time of the year. The mechanics of how super tempests are generated is a scientific marvel. The cascading effect of temperature gradients and pressure gradients and a number of other lower and upper atmosphere parameters contribute to the birth of a storm. The verse penned here is a reflection on this event.

A blistering sun beats down remorseless,

The land parched, every grain of heated sand,

Sucks dry the moisture rendering the sky cloudless,

Mirage shimmers of ascending thermals in seamless band,

Rise to the cool ramparts seeking a celestial rest,

Nature's invisible conduit of suction at its behest.

The waters of the ocean in silent turmoil froth and fume,

Lather whipped up by sub-sea currents, the wind detach,

This vapour stream extracted the heavenly lung consume,

Mushrooming in bellicose vein the nimbus layers attach,

Veritable monster, flexing its muscles steadily grows,

Sheer hunger in its tormented belly, the thunder growls.

The sun in its southern journey bestows a slanted glance,

Cool northern breeze heavy and lazy in wintry slumber,

Is rudely awakened, an invitation to a heated dance,

Swirling in frenzy they meet in an annihilating number,

Resonating the heavenly breath now in crescendo soar,

Passion consummates their ardour in a thundering roar.

LESSON BY THE RIVER

Rivers have always fascinated me. The quite ambience of the pre-monsoon flow to the ravaging floods of the rainy season or the frozen serenity of the winter to the molten icy flow of the early summer, the river was always a dynamic entity, symbolizing change. This poem traces the path of the river from the mountains to the sea. From the time of the early Indus civilization in the Vedic period, the river was the Centre of human progress. This progress was not only economical but also spiritual. Whether it is the Nile or the Euphrates and Tigris or Saraswathi or Ganges, the river basin was the cradle of civilization and the embryo from which all the present knowledge developed.

With a sense of gratitude, I dedicate this verse to my forefathers.

A still reflection in the icy waters the lofty peak,

Clad perennial white wafting cloud and immaculate snow,

From your bosom nature suckled you to feed the torrent,

Glacial feed absorbing the summer and subterranean heat,

Thine immensity built over the eons a constant process,

Locked within a billion year of latent, trapped energy,

The mighty river is but a miniscule and benign display,

Your might ever resting, teasing the sense perception,

The waters descend to the arid plains transformed green,

For many a season replenishing the richness of the soil,

That which you bore from the very depths of thy springs,

An alchemic process deftly deployed to riches transform.

As though by divine appointment the many rivers meet,

Ere the destination in a vast concourse turned quicksilver,

By the fierce rays of the summer sun and a cloudless sky,

The delta is a puzzle to discern its composition and nature,

Is it water flowing on land or a low tide and sand banks,

Like a maiden draped in a white silken robe in the wind,

Your shifting course flaunts the naked moistened earth,

Intoxicated by your beauty I travel in a rugged sail boat,

Seeking and searching for your source and destiny.

Your might humbles my being as timeless you flow,

Constancy of purpose no man made impediment barred,

To the mighty ocean deep, purifying in grand absolution.

You have washed many a sin and conveyed the ashes,

The mortal remains, you have set free the ageless spirit,

A chore aptly bestowed for thou art the chosen candidate,

Signifying eternal presence yet constant change your hue,

I humbly kneel on your banks quench my parched soul,

As the waters of the sea in the warm monsoon currents,

Lifted to the sky residing in the nimbus trace, a path,

Predestined to delight in the embrace of the deities abode,

You submit in totality to reside in the heart of the hills,

Let me likewise lose all identity in this temporal existence,

To be returned to the very font from where I was raised,

So I may in tranquillity be a river to my people.

BURNING BUSH

I had chanced upon an image of a lone Baobab tree against the setting sun's rays in the African savannah thrilled my heart to write this verse. I have visited the vast emptiness of the Arizona desert. I have seen the tall cactus that provides a humbling experience and a lesson in survival but the beauty of this scene took me aback. The thought that first came to my mind was Divine glory reflected through nature. If we all realise this great truth, then the mindless destruction of our forests and natural reserves that has been gifted to us through eons of painstaking growth and nurturing could be stopped.

The bark of the Baobab is useful in papermaking... perhaps, the paper that helps in translating my thought to print comes from the savannah. I will now let your imagination run wild as you read the poem!

In the savannah the golden grass stands tall,

Acres of pure shimmering strands undulate,

Horizon mingling in the sun set this evenfall,

The distant rainbow coloured strata osculate,

Dancing reeds, untold glee in nature's caress,

Clouds ablaze as the diffracted rays ingress.

Every crystalline icicle magnifies the radiance,

Casts a shining beam upon the lonesome tree,

Trunk debarked in a quiet moment of dalliance,

Passing rhinos hone their horn in satiated glee,

Mirrored reflection of the replicated subtle light,

Waltz like glistening fire that burns into the night.

As Moses stood rooted to the hilly terrain,

Witness to the force that singed the lone bush,

A fire that destroys not but of empowering strain,

So am I a lucky spectator in this meadow lush,

Mingling one with beauty that is bestowed,

Transformed is my soul this blessing endowed.

CHEETAH

This piece was inspired by watching a documentary on 'Hunters' in the Discovery Channel in my living room. I did not have the good fortune of travelling to the Serengeti, the habitat of this beautiful and graceful predator. The singular purpose with which the pack hunts down a Thomson Gazelle is a lesson in determination and team playing. While the Cheetah is gifted with burst of speed over a short distance it lacks the stamina of the Gazelle. Nature provides an equal playing field in this game of survival.

On the Serengeti, the Dark Continent sparingly breeds,

A species so lethal yet so graceful and sleek,

Eight feet of sheer power and speed as its pack leads,

Hunting the deer, picking the prey the slow and the weak.

Tall grass ideal camouflage, for the coat pale yellow,

Spots dance to the rhythm of the fluid elegant motion,

Waterhole explodes as the hunted wildebeest bellow,

Earth reverberating frantic stampede and commotion.

The measured steps stealthily employed, the body taut,

Frozen in time like a sculpture, a finely chiselled artefact,

Burning eyes the very embodiment of focus wrought,

The hunter awaits the victim for one erroneous act.

The beast is released as if from a high strung bow,

Twist and turn the trampled grass a magic pattern weave,

Blurred motion culminates jaws holding a struggling doe,

Regal walk trophy claimed, to his brood by the shady tree.

Caring mother the fresh meat to the cubs feed,

Her mate from the hunt returns for the sumptuous feast,

Well-earned rest after many a futile sortie and final deed,

A portrait so aptly depicted this, nature's fastest beast.

COMET VISIT

In August 2001 the Leonid shower was witnessed. As I sat in the open terrace of my home in Chennai, hoping against hope, to witness the shower attenuated by the city lights, I was granted a vision of a few meteor strikes. This was not the fantastic display that was reported in the newspapers the next day. As I sat and contemplated, my consciousness merged with that of the comet Temple–Turtle and this mingling resulted in the verse that follows.

From the icy depths of space a wandering,

A sublimation destined to a fiery end,

I am ensconced in the stillness of a collated mass,

A frigid form, speeding through the firmament,

Tugged by the gravitational pull of the solar mass,

Objects seen and unseen, the universal longing,

Know not that you are on a destructive embrace,

Balanced well on a fabric invisible yet my sojourn,

Mercurial defined eons before in a galactic dance,

I keep faith in the collaborative endeavour,

My form to reshape, yet another cycle of hibernation,

Million miles I traverse in a cosmic cycle of constancy,

I am but a cosmic pebble on a mighty sling,

To launch an elliptical trajectory to the passage,

That brings me nigh the annihilating cauldron,

Sustainer of earthly life, this visitation eagerly awaited,

As the summer heat coaxes the humans to readily shed,

Every vestment, seeking the caress of the cool sea breeze,

I too am drawn, my icy crust to cast away,

Leaving in its wake a lengthy luminous trail,

Blown away, like a jet stream in the upper strata,

The partial immolation a holy act, a pilgrim's ablution,

Ritual of cleansing, ere a visitation to the holy sanctum,

In my ecstasy my hardened shell fragments,

Upon the splendour and glory of the deity's sight,

An apt offering, the denuded elements immersed,

In flaming glory of sacrificial transubstantiation.

To the beholder, I am an anticipated guest,

My blazing glory a blessing bestowed in radiant display.

I now retreat to the cold depths in steady contemplation,

Rejoicing in the thought my existence destined,

Constant cyclic purification until my form,

Transformed to pure energy in eternal unification.

EARTH RISING

From the time of the Apollo mission, one picture that fascinated me was the 'Earth rising' image as taken from the moon. This picture evokes a strong sentiment of gratitude to the home we have. We seem to take for granted this blessing.

Deep contemplation in all-encompassing force that reside,

The illusionary empty space, a warping link establish,

Path defying the known laws of nature, I joyfully decide,

Travel beyond this bondage, to terrestrial gravity banish.

I rise from the mountain my being infinitesimally shrunk,

Subatomic mass with the speed of light, space deformed,

Reach for the destination the silvery orb sunlight drunk,

Cratered terrain a distant cataclysmic event formed.

Like a blossoming flora drenched in the morning dew,

My form restored on the lunar soil, the very cold touch,

Invigorates my soul, the inner form given life grew,

To its full stature begetting human attribute and much.

Unimpeded by polluted air, the perennial night black,

Provides the fitting backdrop to the million sparkling star,

An eerie silence engulfs my body as my ardent search lack,

Answer to this strange milieu from my mortal home far.

To my prayer a comfort seeking, the horizon weaves,

Magic image, a bluish disk brushed wisps of cloud,

Earth rising to greet my lonesome heart and feeling leaves,

Gratitude that the blessing is nigh at home well endowed.

PLANETARY MOTION

A set of Limericks penned in lighter vein on celestial occurrence that conveys deeper meaning, while providing a lighter ambience.

Parallel rays of light do meet at infinity,

Unless you have a Black hole in the vicinity,

Then the truant and defying force of gravity,

Bends these beams in cosmic laxity,

Then beyond the event horizon there is no entity.

Saturn's many rings are asteroid disk,

Trapped too close to the mass by constant frisk,

Many rocks and pebbles at high-speed whisk,

As the Gas giant thwarts the collapsing, collating risk,

Of many moons or some massive fused obelisk.

Mars is the planet they call red,

As man's next destination it is being bred,

Debates and arguments abound with great dread,

There is already a face on the surface well spread,

They say man came from Mars ere this land he tread.

Leonid in celestial display grants a meteor shower,

When in sun's vicinity the splintering comet hover,

The many fragments earthward in this nightly hour,

Descend and as atmospheric friction overpower,

Glow bright in the grandeur of heavenly shower.

I am singed and smouldered by the solar flare,

None will be envious of my proximity to sun's glare,

Constant companion the corona my brilliance ware,

Ridicule not my destiny some day you will better not fare,

All to my fate when granted sun's annihilating stare.

Master of bigamy thirty nine moons you embrace,

Atmosphere of Ammonia and Methane a hostile place,

Turbulent hurricane never quenched your terrain race,

A primordial concoction, the cauldron where life's trace,

Its innocuous beginning our planet to grace.

FLIGHT PATH INTERRUPTED

We are very fortunate to have our house on the flight path of the Little Egrets that inhabit the marshes on the outskirts of the Chennai metropolis in Southern India. Thousands of these birds make it a daily ritual to fly north in the evening and return to their feeding grounds in the early morning. It is an eagerly awaited journey that my wife and I used to witness whenever we were at home. We used to take our evening tea to the open terrace and sit down and await these birds. The observation was an educative experience in teamwork, precision and pure intuition. At times, they fly so low that one can hear the flap of the wings. Some of these experiences are penned as a poem.

The vespers echo on the vaulted ceiling of varied hue,

Melodious tenors and sopranos a group of parakeet,

In celestial flight sway and dance a heady brew,

Imbibing I skyward travel by some cunning deceit.

As the sun's rays crimson tinges the astral lanes,

The southerly sojourn of this convoy is but a prelude,

From the mangrove marshes the Siberian cranes,

Take flight to the salt flats with their entire brood.

Filling the sky with numbers and formation varied,

Unabated beat of the snow white feathered wing,

Shifting, swaying the pattern a congregation serried,

A thousand arrows unleashed from a giant sling.

Wave upon wave, the half-moon playing hide'n seek,

On the thousand wings in perpetual motion

Leaders changing, flight uninterrupted, motion sleek,

Picture of harmony in this world of commotion.

Blessed am I this cerebral tonic daily association,

Gratitude wells up in my heart for this exposition,

Creation, perpetuation and wondrous manifestation,

Life's meaning, change within routine, a substantiation.

MOUNTAIN WALK

This poem was written after a visit to the Western Ghats, a mountain range that runs down the western side of the Indian subcontinent. There is a famous tourist spot called 'Dolphin's Nose,' a few hours' drive from the hill town of Coonoor. This is a very unique rock formation and the route to this spot is wild and scenic. Some of the woods in this region are virgin territory as they are dense and located in precipitous rock face. The path itself, though motorable, is turning and twisting and resembles a cobbled street that lacks maintenance. A few houses that shelter the guardians of the tea plantation break the monotony of the wooded path.

Chirping cicadas raise an undulating chorus on the hill,

Vegetation fertilized through constant drench of moist air,

A steady climb, the foliage break, to reveal a vale to thrill,

The ravine encrusted a tapestry green one's senses stir.

Far from human habitation, the trimmed plantation of tea,

Carpet the precipitous slopes, etched with humble habitat,

Creepers of multi-hued flora break the green monotony,

Silver oaks stand as a welcoming armoury for a diplomat.

The cool mountain air, the resplendent sights I behold,

Arches of mingled branches, the knurled, knotted pattern,

Eroded embankments, exposed roots, in my mind unfolds,

Fantasy reaped by the filtering light as of a magic lantern.

As the cloud lifts from the valley, the distant cascade,

Roars free, a shimmering rainbow on the breaking spray,

Drenches the subservient boulders in a knightly accolade,

Tall grass like kingly subjects genuflect in reverent display.

A simian colony upon the wet rocks matinee council hold,

Elders chatting serious matter ignoring the young of clan,

Who somersault down the slopes and the rocky fold,

In philosophical contemplation an elder landscape scan.

I reluctantly wrench my heart from this happy scene,

The inner spirit detached stays to savour the nectar sweet,

As the honeybee the hidden essence from the flower wean,

My soul suckled by this visitation lags my body in retreat.

THE ORNATE STONE

Most unique rock sculptures that nature carves have stood for millions of years. The sight of this rock formation stoked a creative fire in my mind. Imagination rode a very speedy steed, accumulating a concoction of scenarios, which finally settled down into these words that you are about to read.

This huge monolith stands like an obelisk at the portal,

Some Gallic village to adorn chiselled by a patient nature,

Thousand varied seasons and many generations mortal,

Have passed by, today you are a witness, a silent feature.

I lean close perchance a story to hear from your heart,

The many events that transpired in your august presence,

Every hue and pattern on your skin a textured art,

A hieroglyphics transcribed for progeny's remembrance.

The streaks of ruby, the frozen trickle of splattered blood,

The many battles and skirmishes fought around this mast,

Swords and lances breathing sparks let loose a flood,

Crimson fluid from valiant knights in an encounter past.

The tiny specks of blue the entombed droplets of a tear,

A fair damsel shed upon unbearable separation of a lover,

Helpless you stood mute witness to the countless fear,

Brake forth like the shaken dew from a windswept flower.

I wonder the cause of smooth, resplendent alabaster hue,

Perhaps a hungry, suckling babe fiercely brought forth,

From the young mothers breast droplets of milk few,

As she rested upon you overflowing, in blissful youth.

Your greying skin centuries chiselled by a hundred storm,

Lustrous as the many seasons veiled and wind caressed,

I seek your soul and spirit as permanency's lasting norm,

Prop my sagging frame now with decay impressed.

OVER THE CLOUDS

As a young man, I had been to the Kulu valley in the Himalayas. The unforgettable experience is the morning walk on a cold February day... walking from the Valley towards the snow covered peaks. Though this was not a regular mountaineering exercise, the sheer beauty of the valley covered in a thick blanket of fog and the glistening peaks in the dawn were worth the arduous toil of climbing a few hundred feet. It was biting cold and my limbs ached for the warmth of the fire. And, as my eyes closed after this exhausted climb, I imagined a more salubrious scenario.

I stand aloft the dew-drenched rock,

The clouds swirling at my booted feet,

Moisture seeping through woollen sock,

A shiver runs down my spine to meet,

The nature's rhythm a cosmic lock,

Signifying the common thread that greet,

Every creation, these thousand buds interlock,

Carpeting the mountains this celestial fleet,

Sails into the vale as snow geese flock,

The marshes a veritable source nutrient replete.

This morning is a blessing and absolution,

Darkness dispels and illumines the mind

The radiant sun in its countenance revelation,

Awakes the spirit in every soul in mankind.

The seven hues that merge in light creation,

Segregated through refraction by every layer find,

A celestial dance one of nature's reverberation,

A snapshot to foster for one spiritually inclined,

Details etched a million upheavals in evolution,

I quench my desire in this lofty citadel reclined.

My long flowing tress gently stirs in the updraft,

As the warmth of the sun rarefies the strata,

The cool breeze rises through every rocky shaft,

Akin to the calming, sweet notes of a sonata.

The cloud now swirls as the eddies of a raft,

Scurrying to the rocky shore, nature's ablator,

Seeking refuge, condensing on every leaf, a craft,

To carry a thousand streams to feed the crater,

Now the heat intense, evaporation skyward waft

This perennial subjugation nature's code and charter.

SYLVAN LIGHT

I started my first job in the town of Dandeli, which features on the tourist map of India. The thick forest and the rivers that bisect them are a wonderful visual treat. On weekends, we used to go to the riverbank and sit quietly listening to the sound of the forest and the stream. As the sun started to climb, the rays used to cut through the foliage and cast a mystical light in the overgrowth.

My heart sings the glory this earthy emissary,

A sculpture in patience nurtured with every raindrop,

Life giving, these woods a balanced nursery,

A green monolith divinely planted perennial crop.

The morning mist dances among the creepers,

Gentle caress deftly bestowed every leaf 'n stalk,

Nudging awake the thousand floral sleepers,

Scented breath cast upon the narrow forest walk.

I wander in amazement as the sunlight peek,

Through the green canopy, a translucent veil,

A damsel hiding her lovely countenance seek,

A surreptitious look, this intruder her domain assail.

Bursting upon my vision are these tall giants,

Standing erect like a planted Indian totem pole,

Internally, ringed images the hierarchy paints,

Secret preserved in duty, creation's empowering role.

Rays of the sun pierce the darkened sylvan alleys,

Brilliant marquetry dazzles in the green tinged light,

Veritable feast to the senses brimming in this chalice,

Nature bestowed on this terrain to my immense delight.

Slanted rays of light, diffracted through timbered lattice,

Blazes with intense focus in this murky chamber,

This sabre of the Jedi heals and wielded with no malice,

Purification its purpose, guide to every rambler.

THORNY BUSH

The Acacia tree is very common in the fringes of the arid landscape. The bird resting on this seemingly hostile environment was enough to stoke the fires of imagination. There is a great lesson to be learnt from this virtual scenario. What is a foreboding and treacherous environment for one could be the harbinger of shelter and security to another. This goes to prove that all of creation has a purpose and we should never ever be judgmental whilst determining the utility of any object in this world.

Sinewy limbs stretched and taut, leafless spectre,

Sharp thorns protruding, layer upon layer a lattice,

Nature woven some translucent fabric enticing,

Designed as a perch for a small feathered tenant,

Ably guarded from every prey cocooned well,

In this airy ramparts, savouring the embalming wind,

The morning dew glistens on every ruddy thorn,

Akin to the nectar on the proboscis of a butterfly,

Wild flowers of rare beauty seems to be etched,

On this arid canvas merging with the wilderness,

The Namibian heat transforms every bough,

Into a hallucinating dance dexterously performed,

Peace descends every occupant in these quarters,

Except for a slow waltz to minimize vaporizing heat.

Seeking every little shade sparsely provided,

As the sun climbs to the zenith in merciless punch,

The lizards burrow into the sand in quest of a layer,

Of bearable ambience to spend the day till evenfall,

As the moon rises in a starry sky, a pallid golden orb,

The dunes renovate to a magic carpet heaving,

The thicket is etched against the fractured disc,

Meaningless fractals swallowed by the quicksand,

The lunar blemish vanishes as the night,

In cool misty progress marches on to the morrow.

VANISHING EARTH

The desert is a picture of raw beauty. One tends to think of the desert as a wasteland. In close proximity, the ground realities are life-threatening but the moment you are in the air-conditioned comfort of an aircraft and look down at the desert landscape, an unseen beauty is revealed. The shadows which the ever-shifting dunes create and the caravan's slow march in the scorching sun transform this canvas into a magical picture.

Suspended I lie face down on a magic carpet gliding,

Below a land of green, smooth undulating in the wind,

Monarch hovers over a Narcissus, a steady beat of wing,

Patterns mesmerising merge, a Doppler teasing the mind.

Sweet fragrance of moist earth, blossoms in full bloom,

Field of rice the stalks bent heavy ready for the harvest,

Sacrifice to nourish millions and alleviate earthly gloom,

Seeds return to start new journey at nature's behest.

Transported by some cosmic force, the land barren laid,

Moon shines bright, the subtle shades of the dunes elope,

A caravan makes steady progress seeking oasis or trade,

Arid wind obliterates the remnant traces on shifting slope.

Elevated high, a lone witness of this planet celestial blue,

Setting beyond the horizon, as darkness of night surround,

From this nightmare. I wake in fear, with no tangible clue,

Seeking a meaning, my mind like a galleon run aground.

Debates, discussion and threat, every nation selfish in aim,

Time is short, our only abode in a critical state of demise,

Reckless polluting of our ecosystem, our sustenance maim,

Return to nature and submit and obey the cosmic premise.

A FALLING LEAF

A single autumn leaf resting on this log captured my imagination to write this short poem. Fall is a season that reminds us of the inevitable end every living thing has to encounter. Death is part and parcel of the process of life. Death has great significance and meaning to anyone who looks at the life process from a grander and cosmic perspective. What appears to be an end is actually a new beginning in the eternal cycle of transformation.

Like a cradle gently rocking in the breeze,

From the final throes of life in the trees,

I am detached, floating on a lonely descent,

To the very soil reason for my lofty ascent,

My final resting place for yet another use,

Elements transferred by this seeming refuse.

I am a single strand in this resplendent mat,

Hues deftly patched in a seamless format,

A tapestry of patterns with constant shift,

The autumn wind the reason for this drift,

Dyed into the ground by seasonal permafrost,

A joy to the discerning eyes that nature host.

HOUSE ON THE HILL

A few years ago, we travelled to a hill station in the Nilgris in Southern India, for a few days of quiet relaxation. The room I was staying in had a window that was facing a dilapidated house with crumbling walls and overgrown climbers, snarling every visible brick. The sight of this building was the reason for the poem that you are about to read.

Out of my window, frosted and cold to the touch, I look,

A grey mist blankets the hill, a sombre spectre unfold,

A wasted mansion its shuttered portals sternly rebuke,

Intruding glance, perhaps a multitude of secrets untold,

Interned in its dark chambers and vaults sealed by cobweb,

Deftly woven, spiders wait for a prey in these dark space,

Trap laid for some winged intruder from the shrub,

Pungent pepper lingers in the silky strands a scented lace,

Tall spiny eucalyptus shorn of branches stand like lance,

Arrayed discordant in the battlefield of decimated troop,

Thin ends sway with remnant leaves in an ethereal dance,

Tearing at the roof, a desire to covertly innards snoop.

Taking courage, I walk to the abode of mystery and death,

The wind sensing my approach howls through the pine,

Chill ascends my being, fear freezes my breath,

With laboured step, I climb the hill on a path serpentine.

I stand before the heavy oak doors, the winds scream,

Through every nook and crevice in the shuttered panel,

Taking courage, I swing open the door and beheld a beam,

Pure white light streaming down an illuminating channel.

Then it dawned on my numbed senses, the mist had lifted,

The sun breaking free cast its rays through a cruciform,

From behind altar wall, imagined a past as faithful drifted,

Life thriving in a more healthy climate and yielding farm.

This fallacy of thought, the illusionary proposition,

Born of ignorance and fearful mind churning of emotion,

Akin to the ray that transformed my very perception,

seeking wisdom to dispel my darkness and commotion.

DAL LAKE

For centuries, writers have used the words, "Paradise on Earth" to describe Kashmir's snow-capped mountains, mirror like lakes, flower gardens, fruit orchards, pine forests, rushing rivers, green valleys and fragrant meadows.

Despite soldiers with body armour and automatic rifles patrolling the streets of the summer capital, Srinagar, it is possible for a tourist to spend a peaceful day floating in a shikara, or gondola, on Dal Lake. The lower Himalayas are reflected in the glasslike, shallow waters. Dabchicks, with their stunted wings, giggle and scoot among the lily pads. From morning to night, town's people row their slim, pointed shikaras across the lake, bearing mounds of lily roots and green reeds for their cows, or seaweed to fertilise Srinagar's floating vegetable and flower gardens. At sunset, they sing. The sight of flowers being carried in the Shikara evoked many thoughts that have been given shape and substance through this poem.

On the placid waters, the Shikaras glide a slow paddle,

Lone oarsman deftly poised transfers the crafted oar,

Pushing through drifting water lilies this wooden cradle,

Rocking gently in the ripples today a sweet cargo store.

The lake refreshed every summer through glacial feed,

Now in a stage of decadence polluted by the essence,

Life exposed to the vagaries of political gain and need,

Reflects the resentment and stink of unholy presence.

Whither the floral tribute destined I query in my mind,

A nuptial chamber to adorn, a union to celebrate,

Or a parting, a décor to the coffin some comfort find,

Decay hangs in the air as distant guns reverberate.

Flowers ever bloom in the vale, sweet scented breath,

Perchance natures remedy to bleach the cordite stench,

Or abundance to fragrance the putrid flesh in death,

Fill not with troops but your plantation every trench.

PILLARS OF HOYSALA

I visited the Hoysala temples in Belur and Halebidu a few years ago. It was an exhilarating experience, a blend of pure aesthetics and an age-old sculptural marvel that seems to defy time. The Hoysala dynasty from the 11th century lasted for two hundred and fifty years. They developed sculptural and architectural styles that were radically different than those that were in existence. The temple scheme is repeated in multiples of two and three. The plinth and sanctum are star-shaped. A wide pathway runs around the temple on the outside for ritual of circumambulation. Horizontal lines and mouldings subdue the tower. It also has miniature-sculptured shrines, fretted string-courses and mouldings. The star-shaped plan of the temple contributes to a greater variety of light and shade. Every part of these temples exhibits a joyous exuberance of fancy, scorning mechanical refrain. All that is wild in human faith or warm in feelings is found portrayed in these temples. As a monument of phenomenal concentration, superior technical skill, ingenuity, imagination and profound religious consciousness of those concerned in their creation, there is no parallel to these anywhere in the world.

Your creation a mighty collaboration nature born,

You lay silent many centuries in the very depths,

Perhaps, a prayer constantly murmured in your heart,

Awaiting a resurrection a better purpose to serve.

Your discovery a discerning artisan's immense delight,

Raised from the earthly womb by a thousand hands,

The unseen umbilical perennially tied to your mother,

The gravity anchoring your sculpted soaring form,

No artificial cement impeding the cosmic energy flow,

Seeded were you by a celestial visitor, a fiery entry,

Compacted and composed for a divine purpose,

You stand a silent testimony, the ordained protector,

The place of worship, revelling in the daily chimes,

Of temple bells, dancer's beat and devotional chants,

The sculptor vigilantly studied your very soul,

While he worked on your purpose and purification,

Octagonal multiples of absolute perfection deemed fit,

Every corner purveyor of the abundant cosmic energy,

Channelled through crystal lattice, your monolithic core,

Multitude of you standing in unmoving faith, succour,

To the million devotees who in admiration stand,

You have been a sentinel to the Kama and Karma,

Of Deities and humans, a symbol of permanence,

The holy emblem of divine peace and tranquillity.

TALKING STONES

The female form in the temples of Hoysala, the dancers, the courtesans and the deities seem to bring to life the erotic energy of the age. As I stood rooted to the floor admiring the intricacies of the sculpture and the eye for detail of the artisan, I was transported back in time and moment into the very soul of the author of these beautiful carvings.

I chanced upon this holy edifice hidden by garments green,

Jewel in the wooded terrain, frozen in space and time,

My eyes closed, hear the multitude of chisels that wean,

From every stone a beauty adorable, alive and sublime,

On a column a buxom maiden applies a mark of beauty,

Tassels and scanty skirt seem to sway in the Deccan wind,

In her very posture one can discern her temporal duty,

The consort, the king's pleasure to enhance determined,

Rain God has coveted her body with a long moist caress,

Drops still linger on her heavy breasts, a hesitant perch,

Running down her long flowing jasmine scented tress,

Knotted skirt parting at the hip clings as a hungry leech.

Every plaque depicts the varied feminine charm and grace,

Echo of the spirit that resides in the unfathomed depth,

Each and every creation, God's serene resting place,

Evoking a kaleidoscope of emotions of unbound wealth.

Lower ramparts are arrayed armoured warriors in battle,

Marching to consummate the emperor's conquering quest,

Roving eyes bring to life soldiers and their sabres rattle,

Intent upon the royal task resting only in conquest.

Meaning well portrayed that through a hundred wars,

Constant struggle empires built, so too these temple walls,

Hours of constant toil created by the hands of many scars,

I offer a salutation to the Divine in whom nature enthrals.

SITTING ON A BENCH

Norwich, in East Anglia, England is almost a second home for my wife and me. This is where our daughter lives and we have been travelling to this beautiful town every summer. On one of these visits, as I was sitting in the town centre in one of those numerous benches you find located at vantage points, these thoughts welled up in my mind.

Sitting on a well-crafted wrought iron bench,

I munched on my tuna sandwich for my lunch,

This was amidst the flow of gaily-attired Norwich folk,

And the pigeons, for morsels, in anticipation flock,

The chilling breeze descends from the North Sea,

Mercilessly sweeps through every lane and tree,

The mini whirlwind on the cobbled stones dance,

The swirl of fallen leaves and litter prance.

The street musician on his battered guitar play,

A melancholy song, a manifestation, a way,

To tell the world his predicament and sad story.

In this town enriched with eventful history.

The mass of humanity on a listless frenzied flow,

Fed on a compulsive need the commerce to grow,

A ritual of visitation stroked by need of perceived joy,

Trapped in a rodent wheel, a consumerist ploy.

I hear the chime of the distant church bell,

A timely warning, a reminder, a death knell,

For all to pause and hear, heart and mind lift,

To slow down, look inward and arrest this drift.

Perhaps the eddies I see and the dried drifting leaf,

A potent meaning for all to refocus a new belief,

Contentment in what we have, a time to reflect,

Human nature, our inner cosmos fathom and protect.

A WALK IN THE PARK

"Like Sleeping Beauty's Palace, the gothic beauty of Norwich's Plantation Garden has been protected from the ravages of time by dense brambles. Step down a narrow drive between two prosperous-looking Victorian villas just outside the city's medieval walls and, as if by magic, you find yourself at the edge of a steep-sided, verdant valley which is in fact a three-acre sanctuary from the hustle and bustle of nearby shopping streets. "Extract from an article by Ms. J Owen, Garden section of The Times October 28, 2000. I wrote these lines sitting in the garden.

Hidden from view, nestling in a large burrow,
I witness a gurgling brook that steadily furrow,
Drawn as though by a magnet I descend the banks green,
Spread out before mine eyes a vast concourse glean,
Wean my senses and bear my being to a heavenly realm.
Acres of green, tall graceful trees, a catacomb of creepers,
Flowers of a thousand hues, every blade the weepers,
Drenched and burdened the frost melting glistening jewel,
Amidst the gracious flora I seek a perennial place to dwell,
My thoughts applaud the caring hands this venue built.
A brocade of crafted stone merged with ornate bricks,
Lattice of green climbers atop the stonewall frolics,
Bringing this ancient edifice by some time warp,
Modern yet history etched in every feature sharp,
In wonder if I could discern a meaning in all I behold.
A Gothic fountain in this garden shaped as a steeple,
Blackened marble mature with the touch of many people,
The water now a trickle signifying the decay of life,
Evokes a sense of gratitude for the focus in its strife,
perform one's duty with diligence in this existence.
The Lilacs, Foxgloves and the bright orange Poppies,
Strewn around this domain as some master's trophies,
A backdrop of ascending steps arrayed as if for a parade,
Interposed lances of yellow, red, pink and many a shade,
Silently I watch the march of time that stood still for long.

TINTERN ABBEY

Walter de Clare founded this abbey, in Monmouthshire, England, in 1131 for the Cistercian monks, who came from the Abbey of Aumone, in the Diocese of Chartres, itself founded only ten years before. Walter's son, Gilbert, first earl of Pembroke, and probably also his grandson Richard Strongbow, conqueror of Ireland under Henry II, were buried at Tintern, the magnificent church, which dates from the end of the thirteenth century. The ruins of Tintern, which stands on the right bank of the river Wye, backed by a semicircle of wooded hills, ranks with Fountains Abbey in Yorkshire as the most beautiful in England. The church, measuring 245 feet in length, with transepts of 110 feet, is almost perfect, though roofless, the architecture being of the transitional style from Early English to Decorated. The window-tracery is especially fine. Hardly anything remains of the domestic buildings of the abbey, the stone having been used for cottages and farm buildings in the neighbourhood. I visited the ruins along with my wife and Janet, who was living in Bath.

As I round the bend in the wooded lane,

The abbey breaks upon the beholder, a blessing,

Aptly bestowed, from the forested terrain,

Tranquillity descends the soul faith professing.

Meandering past the cloister wall,

The river gurgles in muted, whispering tone,

A baptismal ablution to cleanse the human fall,

Gifted in this Eden to restore the seed sown.

I stand rooted to the floor facing the altar bare,

Multitude of thoughts arise in my tormented mind,

Hear the chant Gregorian, perhaps the Matins fare,

praying, hooded against the chilling wind.

Restful abode in spiritual pursuit, secluded life,

Benedictine rules self-imposed, seeking supplication,

A cleansing of the heart from every worldly strife,

Mission to gain in temporal life divine replication.

Edifice in decay, the roof ripped open to the sky,

Skeletal remains of yesteryears echoing the fortitude,

Worship performed in ardent toil and comfort deny,

of the unimpeded deluge of beatitude

.

BEAUTIFUL LYNTON

Lynton & Lynmouth are two villages in Devon on the coast of the Bristol Channel. One is at the top of the hill the other is at the bottom; there is a cliff railway, which can be used to commute between these two villages. From atop the hill, breath taking views are to be found overlooking the Bristol Channel to Wales across the other side of the water.

I have visited these shores on two occasions but find something new every time I went back. This corner of England has an unadulterated beauty.

The winding road climbs the manicured hills,

Rolling countryside, dotted with farms and cattle pen,

Rising dense mist the Bristol Bay gurgles and chills,

The lissom damsel on the shores of beautiful Devon.

In the warm current the Sea Gull glides,

A rocky perch to seek where young ones roost,

Fresh catch on its painted bill secure resides,

Above the cacophony as boisterous residents joust.

The sheer drop of the cliffs seem to draw out,

By some immense suction the rocky landscape,

My exposed face flushed as if by some viral bout,

I sit on the boulder nature's captive loath to escape.

Your beauty ensnared the romantics like Shelly,

Upon the banks of Lyn his love did profess,

Tempestuous river catalyst of passion flow freely,

Unfettered you roam every impediment transgress.

Narrow path leads to the valley of the Rocks,

A granite cathedral perched high above the sea,

Genuflecting nimble footed goats in woolly frocks,

Pay obeisance to your soaring spirit upon their knee.

Seeping waters innocuously drained from the moor,

Imperceptible origin, a firm gush, a perpetual cataract,

A scintillating orchestra, a festooned audience lure,

Witness to the confluence, your final act.

CASTLE REST

My wife and I took a holiday in North Wales during the summer of 1997. Our daughter chose the destination for us. It was the Bodelwyddan Castle. The stately rooms, the rolling acreage of woodland and the structure itself were awe-inspiring. I do not want to spend much time on the historic details of the castle as this information is available in plenty in books, tour guides and the Internet. Read on the thoughts that galloped like the knights of yore during this visit.

Dragons breathing fire, knights riding high,

Shining armours, damsels in distress heaving sigh,

My imagination like a stallion, wild and rampant fly,

To the time when the ramparts and the lofty belfry,

Were built to the need and vanity of a proud prince,

Long interned his might deeds and conquests since,

Immortalised but these weathered stones wince,

Constant attention desire for past blemish rinse.

The turrets like gleaming trumpets skyward raised,

Mist swirling as cold wind the heated vapour fused,

A ghostly revelation dancing to my mind dazed,

The moon breaks free and my fears erased.

As I lay my head in this ornate chamber royal,

Where perhaps the valet and soldiers loyal,

Rested their scarred frame and planned to foil,

Encroaching enemy, to save their prince and soil.

The monolith stands witness to the purpose built,

Long lost its intent, a slow ablution of varied guilt,

Transcend in intent to joy providing up to the hilt,

Doorman stands majestically clad in Scottish kilt.

It is my transitory abode, respite and pleasure seeking,

Tranquil in nature, the summer sun quietly peeking,

The distant nimbus flashing and thunder reeling,

Ensconces my tired limbs, rest to my body aching.

CONFLUENCE

It was a cool afternoon in the historic town of Dartmouth. I was impressed with the colourful old buildings and incredibly scenic landscapes. In addition to its many famous adventurous citizens, including Francis Drake, Walter Raleigh and John Davis, Dartmouth is known to history as the port in which the Pilgrim Fathers aboard the Mayflower and Speedwell stopped for repairs and outfitting before sailing from nearby Plymouth for America. As I sat on the riverbank in the town and looked towards the sea, where the Dartmouth Fort stands and the river meets the sea, these thoughts came over me.

I have watched a multitude of civilisation flourish,

Fed by my alluvial treat and my gentle moist touch,

Have borne galleons of trade, joyous men with relish,

Jealously guarded my course from invader's clutch.

The long journey, a unique identity soon to end,

I wind down the valley of rare beauty of celestial make,

Levees in garments of habitation, to my destiny send,

A silent salutation to my life's deeds, a funeral wake.

In the orient, the dearly beloved send crafted gift,

To soul departed to a new abode, deserving the best,

A hundred masts stripped of sail and flag, nod and lift,

life ebbs into the vastness of the ocean ever to rest.

I behold the villas and homes a sign of wealth and toil,

Standing at my wake, bidding a richly deserved stay,

My life's good work discharged for betterment of soil,

My gratitude for your thought and the tribute you pay.

I caress the castle ramparts centuries rooted in my depth,

Like a lover's lingering glance, deeply implanted kiss,

My emotions surge and eddies break in many a death,

The calm descends as my spirit rests in eternal bliss.

The Gods of the sea roar their approval in the surf,

As in this confluence a life ends and another newly born,

A part of me is returned in the rising tide to the old turf,

To enrich the might Oak and the germinating acorn.

ON THE DART

Janet, our friend who moved to Totnes from Bath, my wife and I spent the entire day cruising on the River Dart in the summer of 2001. The cruise starts from Totnes and goes up to Dartmouth. It returns in the evening to Totnes. The route of this meandering river is steeped in history and the bird life is exotic. The vineyards and the estates, of the rich and famous, glide past the boat in quick succession. My experience of the journey finds an outlet in the following poem.

Fed by the many rivulets from the highland on the moor,

Waltzing around the ancient rocks and exposed roots,

Enticing whisper, the bubbling echo, an enchanting allure,

Draws the bees and the heavy plumaged egrets to roost,

The flaming Kingfisher sits on the aged and knurled oak,

Focus intent on some targeted prey in the water marked,

Hovering in sharp focus, with tiny wings unabated stroke,

A dive and reward retrieved, an effortless chore embarked,

Cradling high on the bank nest woven on a lonely pine,

A pair of ospreys an early summer visitor to this domain,

Circle in search of ample feed in the forested ravine,

A new brood to start and high perch for warmth to gain.

River widens in the estuary ere its seaward destination,

The multitude of tides twists and turns a relentless force,

Akin to a Boa unleashing a strike this watery incarnation,

Seethes and surges, every age a new pattern and course.

The thick foliage of Elms and Oaks carpet the slope,

The watermark denudes the branches and trunk debarked,

Nature's craft, a telling record or perchance a ray of hope,

For some marooned mariner a misadventure embarked.

Illustrious personnel their estates cherished and own,

Agatha's plots of villains were hatched on your bank,

Wines from your estates has the accolade of the crown,

Tranquil you flow lest awake those in your bosom sank.

AUTUMN COLOURS

I have had the good fortune of travelling through the Rhine valley as well as through the North East of the United States during the autumn. The colours of autumn have always captivated me. The nippy chill in the air, the falling leaves and the colours have added a magical touch to my travels.

Shades of crimson red brushed against the amber,

Thick sinews erupting from the soft yielding soil,

Dense mist of myriad hue, the brightly glowing ember,

Lights up this sylvan canvas a great artist yearly toil.

Bright green leaves that fed on the summer sun,

Precious heat percolating through million vein,

Every pore life's breath emanating and respite shun,

Chill pant of decay now in the aching limbs ingrain.

The autumn rings the death knell bitter and sweet,

Foliage resplendent, the gladiator's bloody vest,

Draped in reverence ere the descent earthly meet,

Phase to nourish the bountiful soil at nature's behest.

I stand in admiration entombed in this golden casket,

Drifting in the numbing breeze multi- hued caress,

A single rubicund leaf rests a cordless locket,

Upon my heaving chest, a symbolic blessing impress.

MANNEQUIN EYES

I had been to Japan a number of times. Though the purpose of visit was business, I had been entertained by my Japanese host in some of the very ethnic restaurants in the Ginza in Tokyo. The delectable part of an evening is not the food itself but the surreal atmosphere created so exquisitely by the serving maidens. The calm posture, the subtle movements and heady scents that accompany them are an experience one never forgets. To those wonderful ladies I dedicate this poem.

On the tatami I sat cross-legged in reverence,

The aroma of richly brewed tea wafting gentle,

Incense sticks pouring forth spiral fragrance,

A trap laid for my spirit in encircling cellulose mantle.

I hear the rustle of footsteps on the wooden floor,

Stolen glance reveals a diminutive damsel,

Clad in kimono, silken robe of exquisite décor,

Sweeping train of fabric, a subtle music propel.

Cherry blossoms carpet the sky,

Azure blue canvas etched floral pattern white and pink,

Every window adorned, branches exuding a sigh,

Perfume enhanced in a heady mix my soul to sink.

A goddess she was extracting my very essence,

Her beauty deftly hidden her face a painted mask,

Those eyes held me captive in her presence,

She sat by my side in service to accomplish her task.

The archer stood in meditation deep focus beget,

The bow raised and the dart placed strung taut,

The arrow released impeccable finds its target,

Piercing through veiled layers this impenetrable fort.

A flicker of her lovely eyes my ardour sweep,

Those mannequin eyes condemns me to prison sweet,

For life, I am enslaved my bliss boundless leap,

I raise my cup of leafy brew, this abode of joy replete.

MALACCAN MELODY

I had visited many towns in Malaysia, including the beautiful island of Langkawi. The town of Malacca had a special impact on me. The multi-ethnic culture, the colourful history of the town and its surrounding provoked me to write this poem.

This Sunday morn fresh and awash after a showery night,

I don my best and take a trip to the south-western coast,

A journey wherein I sit and watch the tall palm's flight,

On the window of my car, to my eyes, a green toast.

Ancient town of Malacca is my destination anticipated,

Soaked in history, every turn and twist a story to tell.

Eons of commerce this little tropical port participated,

Today contributions in acquired souvenirs the town sell.

Walking the narrow alleys, the Chinese settlers paved,

I close my eyes and travel to the past, the rickshaws rattle,

Ornate vestibules, the nobility and mendicant craved,

Rest the weary legs in many sorties of life's diurnal battle.

High ceilings decorated with chandeliers Victorian,

To intruders slyly watch, Peep hole in sleeping chamber,

The hand cranked music box playing chants Gregorian,

Heady scent of aromatic oils, burnt incense and camphor.

The arching dragons and the sun backed tiles on the roof,

Supported by the dovetailed rafters cleverly employed,

A symbol of life's heavy burden and early trader's proof,

A life with nature merged and acumen wisely deployed.

The mouth-watering summer fruits, a meal of curry rice,

Rows of bull horned houses adorned with fragrant trees,

The sea breeze gently wafting, to mix the smell of spice,

The hard existence, these simple pleasures, frees.

The Dutch quarters painted in rich earthy brown,

Perchance to hide the tobacco spittle and scorn,

Or an arrogant symbol of total dominance of the crown,

Today a testimony well preserved for the future born.

On the hill, the ramparts safely guard the catholic edifice,

Remnants of sacrilegious intent and conqueror's attitude,

Testimony to the pioneering spirit of the Portuguese,

A monument, a living symbol of faith and fortitude.

MIRRORED WATER

Any romantic will be fascinated by Venice, the art connoisseur's paradise, with its serpentine waterways and grandiose architecture. This poem traces a path into the very soul of Venice, a journey into its past and the various events that shaped its splendour.

Mirrored in the intruding waters this city glory shuns,

Abode so beloved of Byron that verse precipitate,

You have been the darling coveted by the Huns,

Assignation, to many a trader this Adriatic port.

Crusades enshrined greed for goods Levantine,

Barbarous occident's appetite goaded to consume,

Cotton, silk, Muslin, exotic glassware and porcelain,

Your very air smells of Indian spice and exotic perfume.

You had instilled a raging passion in every Venetian,

Annual ritual the Dodge your virtuous essence wed,

Matrimonial band cast into the sea at tide's depletion,

Patricians jealously governed and thine fame spread.

Plato's republic adopted with tantalising change,

A cultural confluence, philosophies richness share,

Pleasant and rich milieu through multi-ethnic exchange,

Righteousness your forte and quality of life your fare.

Opera domiciled in every artefact marble and mahogany,

Three centuries from a subtle beginning in Monteverdi,

Rich concoction Instrumentation, sequence and harmony,

Novel intro of counter-tenor, merciful end to the Castrati.

Your fame so impressed the Victorian bard,

A famous play he did pen to mercy invoke,

When nature perished the bounty to your dockyard,

To every reader, even stone hearted, a tear provoke.

Oh! Venice your Gondolas the waterways glide,

To the lovers you bestow an enchanting serenade,

Tribute I pay in remembrance this historical ride,

For mirrored in the water, your glory resplendent parade.

ESCAPE FROM BODMIN

On travel around the north coast of Devon, I had visited Maidenhead, Lynton, Ilfracombe and Combe Martin. In the south I had visited Totnes, Plymouth, Dartmouth and Exeter. The whole region was notorious for its smuggling activity in the eighteenth century. Jack Rattenbury was a smuggler who operated the south coast. This is a true-life account in verse.

Taken prisoners on the way to the cells in Bodmin,

To quench their thirst they halted at the "India Queen,"

While the warders were downing their potation,

Jack bribed the coach hands in small denomination.

Upon the command of the inebriated constables,

The horses were reigned marched from their stables,

Refusing to alight the coach, an uproarious scuffle ensued,

Trading blows, bullets streaking, help sought and refused,

The drivers said, their duty to mend the stallion,

No partaking in law enforcement by the battalion,

Under cover of darkness, through a garden gate,

Escaped into the woods Jack and his prison mate.

Hiding in the trenches in the chill of the wintry night,

Saw a man approaching, every breadth held in fright,

Relief dawned like a refreshing awakening state,

When his name was called and found that it was his mate.

Travelling through the night chanced upon a reverend,

Who took them to Newkey and ten sterling did lend,

Taking a boat the direction of the wind cleverly employ

Reached Beer to his loving wife and everyone's joy.

SMUGGLERS OF DEVON

A man called Jack Beven hailed from Devon,

Folks thought he was a gift of God from heaven,

As coast to coast he in benevolence roam,

His riches bestowed upon many a charity home,

His inheritance was from a smuggler of Ilfracombe.

There was a smuggler called Sydney,

Whose life style led to the loss of a kidney,

His days were numbered and his health crumble,

On his deathbed could scarcely mumble,

He's hid his wealth behind a thicket of bramble.

A fearsome four on the inn's door bang,

Muskets handy and polished armour clang

The inmates knew the callers as Press gang,

Men from the cutter that called at Isle of Lundy,

Knew that this was their last free mond'y.

Drinking tea became a gracious English custom,

Due to the many crates that went past the Custom

Thanks to the gallant men of the Severn Sea,

Today we have to import many more crates of tea.

An honest trader once sailed "The Bristol Galley,"

Settled Down under and had a plantation of Sallee,

For he knew not that all pilots ran contraband.

His reputation is now perennial marred as a brigand.

There was a landlady at "The Jolly Sailor,"

Who went by the name of Carrie Jo Tailor,

To hide from a search party, a keg of brandy,

She sat on the barrel akimbo, a machete handy,

Many thought it cute but some thought it randy.

Perhaps you ought to know of Jack Corlyon of Coverack,

Many engaged his skills, to build boats on contract,

But he went to sea with a cargo of contraband,

He left his favourite red shirt on the land,

So when the coast was clear and his men landing man'd,

His wife would hang out his shirt to dry on the strand.

Jack Rattenbury was born at Beer,

Ere he came into the world he lost his father dear,

Went to sea at nine, tutored by his uncle to fish,

Lost the rudder and his mentor did sincerely wish,

He learnt at someone else's expense,

So to Brixham trawler it will be hence,

Learning quick and onto larger vessel volunteering,

Jack decided that his future lay in privateering.

A historical place of worship, the Salcombe church,

Had many a pastor on the pulpit sway and lurch,

For it was known as the hideout for the Mutters,

The contraband spirit sampled led to stutters,

Of the Deacons, the custodian of spiritual matters.

Salcombe's sexton the famous Robert Channon,

Was a doctor of the church and knew every canon,

Of worldly matters, he knew Abraham Mutter,

Behind his Bar at Exmouth he is sure to be,

If not Bob knew he was running contraband at sea.

A SHELTER OF LOVE

Your countenance radiates warmth,

In purifying grace you divinely bestow,

Protection for body, mind and soul,

In this cruel world of loveless solitude,

You the tabernacle in which resides,

Love personified, true divine image.

Innocence born with no malice,

Nurtured homeless in grime and filth,

The web of insensitivity a trap cast,

No hope to break free till you dawned,

Like the nourishing Sun in their lives,

Casting light in their darkened lives.

Your care and concern daily bestows,

Silken threads to weave a cocoon,

A SHELTER of immeasurable love,

Nurtured thus, this flock transforms,

To vibrant citizens a metamorphosis,

Of empowerment in this journey!

A SOLITARY CLOUD

Golden rays of the dawn breech,

A solitary moisture laden swell,

Fluffy cotton candy out of reach,

Evolving shapes in hurried travel,

It's origin a terrestrial crucible,

Elevated by the vaporising heat,

To the cool firmament invisible,

Colossal suspension in retreat,

In a cycle perpetual in nature,

Purifying in ever loving nurture.

A WALK BY THE LAKE

Stillness pervades the green grassy meadow,

The water undulating, a tumultuous expanse,

Silvery glimmer in a play of light and shadow,

Stirred by the breeze, as the surface glance.

Exploding pods cast into the air winged seed,

Drifting in the waft like unsullied snowflakes,

Destination unknown, yet some purpose lead,

Harbinger of life, a way nature laid it partakes.

Lodged in some crevice, a rocky outcrop below,

Nurtured by the rain drops or condensing dew,

Sprouting to be a carpet of Dandelion yellow,

Delight to the beholder, the discerning few.

The water lilies pink dance to the gentle waves,

Fens on shore weave intricate pattern in sway,

Nectar sucking swallow tail the gusts braves,

Unmindful of the competing honeybees in foray.

I love the walk by the lake a soothing beatitude,

An enchanted ambience, a portal to the Divine,

Like the winged seed I take flight in solitude,

To the shores beyond the tangled mind of mine.

BEYOND THE TURMOIL

I wonder why the mind, a twisted journey takes,

For some trivial purpose, a self-satisfying construct,

Imaginary hurdles, unfathomable chasms it makes,

A knotted mess, the state of intended joy to destruct.

Like a fine meshed sieve, the granulated feelings ill,

Retained, aggregated and glued by incessant negativity,

A gravitating mass one's being incrementally fill,

Oppressing weight leading to a paralysis of all creativity.

The mind in ego mode is an ill equipped unstable toy,

Poised like a spinning top, a false stability in motion,

Toppled by any subtle variant that emotions employ,

Temporary stability of lunacy in numbing commotion.

Immobile is its structure when materially beached,

Rough edges honed, balanced to a spherical frame,

A gliding mind focused, easily its purpose reached,

In this many manifestations temporal, a divine game.

Now empty the turbulent mind of all gravitating dross,

Lighten my mind's burden, an ascending path to trace,

Let many Masters' wisdom aid me, the horizon to cross,

Beyond this sea of turmoil, I await your eternal embrace.

BLUE JOHN CAVERN

Rolling hills with green pasture the nourished sheep feed,

Slopping hill acute leads to the a shallow denuded dell,

Stone walls juxtaposed, a protected arena shield,

Revealed by some eager prospector, this deviant swell,

Did evince interest for an search, find a treasure store,

Or a smuggler's ware, a well worth toil to explore.

Hard toil, a dig over many years does reveal a cavern deep,

Nature etched in slow labour over many a thousand year,

Many veins run deep in this abyss, a vast domain sweep,

Alleyways of jagged rocks etched for a pressure relief clear,

Subterranean flow, rampant fury, finds a tortuous route,

Akin to the display of an infuriated and unleashed brute.

Inner sanctum, surreal decked by extruded stalactite flute,

Andesite flutes adorned in multihued, shimmering veil,

Ages the fluorite collated, illuminate the narrow chute,

Large chamber opens within the labyrinth, a place to hail,

Venting persistent pressure, a pause in this geological toil,

Churning the rocky debris to shape the walls a helical coil.

Lanes branch from this central hall, opens a narrow shaft.

Closing in a crypt of sparkling walls, soaring to the dome,

Blue tinged sinew of rare fluorspar an embedded graft,

Eons of elemental accretion to find an implanted home,

Priceless treasure a captive in this cavern, a sacred berth,

Lying dormant in its lustre awaiting to be unearthed.

CAPTIVE IN THE ROARING OCEAN

The maiden on the forepeak looks out into the expanse,

Intended guardian of this vessel against nature's wrath.

Inbuilt protector lacking in Ulysses mighty Aegean craft,

Song of Sirens cast a spell, a magical trance the aftermath.

Sails torn the ship charges the treacherous rocky outcrop,

Drifting from its course orchestrated by the siren's wail,

Deceptive, veiled silken voices to entice, caution to drop,

Disaster for the crew and craft wrought by the aimless sail.

Gone are the tales of mythical maidens, this ocean voyage,

A ship, sails unfurled, catches the benevolent easterly,

Steady pace in the calm sea makes an uneventful passage,

Makes progress, jaunty sailors rollick on the deck leisurely.

ADRIFT IN THE OCEAN

I searched for the distant shore for an abode of hope,

The raging sea pummels my raft of loosely tied timber,

A lantern secured to the mast sways on tattered rope,

Straining through the intense foam the vision hinder,

Burning eyes from the salt spray as vision blurs,

Intense darkness descends on the weary frame,

Clinging to the boards I lie holding on to the oars,

By a miracle a land to reveal an island with no name.

CITY STREAKS

Limericks in lighter vein

A notorious jewel thief of Minneapolis
Evaded every attempt of the Minnesota police
Like a stealthy cat he did the disappearing act
Until his hand got caught in a crystal artefact,
He is now cooling his heels in cell in Acropolis.

There was a man from Budapest
Who in society was an incessant pest
In public he would latch on like a leech
And high morals and sermons he would preach
When he passed away they buried him in a steel chest
There was an oarsman from Calcutta

Who took part in the annual regatta
He took a wrong turn in the Sunder bans
Got trapped in the shallow sand banks
Years later he was found in the lower strata

There was a gentle man from Milan

Who impeccably dressed with élan

Every crease and fold in proper place

A picture of poise and starched grace

Many said he was no human but an automaton.

There was a devout Christian of Rome

Who for many years lived in a catacomb

He never knew the fall of the empire

His progeny in the labyrinth did expire

Their ghosts the subterranean paths roam.

COSMIC ORCHESTRATOR

Celestial composer whose enchanting melodies enslave,

My soul in rapture to imbue the quenching nectar deep,

From the slumber of worldly woes which I daily brave,

Bestow the wisdom, the inhibiting layers to leap.

Consciousness dimmed as the needle's eye, empty dictate,

Splintered thoughts rooted in fragmenting duality,

A fathomless abyss of interning desire my being abdicate,

Intuitive capacity for reflection tainted to opaque quality.

Music of your reed penetrate my soul's deflecting wall,

Emanation of your flute a vibration of wisdom manifold,

My soul longs for divine embrace, an ecstasy to enthral,

Reveal thine infinitude and undo my hindering blindfold.

Gopis hear the divine sound and foretells your presence,

Worldly bonds they forsake as their spirit soar and dilate,

Every creature's purpose, bridal union, in your essence,

In all creation you, the playmate and the causal substrate.

You, the cosmic orchestrator, of the chaos that pervade,

As the perpetual whirling cosmic dancer, order reinstate,

Multitude of harmonious forms pour in endless cascade,

You are the unbroken thread of the cosmic fabric intricate.

Your universal form to your ardent seeker you did reveal,

Mortal eyes thine lustre cannot behold hence inner sight,

Ignite the consuming Divine spark, this my appeal,

To merge in your cosmic dance, formless in your light.

DANCING NORTHERN LIGHTS

The ghostly apparition dances in the sky,

A mesmerizing act of supple movements,

In Solar realms, imperceptible tempests fly,

The corona dilated in twisting torments,

Fiery arches ebb and seethe in eerie silence,

Unseen the tentacles reach out into space,

Now in Solar embrace and lively resilience,

A participation in a ballet of visual grace.

Your green hue and unfettered bold stroke,

Against the canvas of the darkness bright,

From the tepee ascends the wafting smoke,

Fire lit for warmth in the cold Arctic night,

Attempts to append the splendour celestial,

Yet the frigid air sucks out the very soul,

Of this added intent in a diffusion terrestrial,

Untainted your dynamic vision is held whole.

Oh! Bright lights that evoke awe and wonder,

Constant token of the protection you impart,

Life giving Sun when it's darker side ponder,

We are shielded by our multi-layered rampart,

We genuflect in gratitude on this icy ground,

To the adept cosmic artisan who did interlace,

Complex patterns in life's expression so sound,

These lights make our soul long for Divine embrace.

DEEPLY ETCHED MEMORIES

On my mind's wall hang many a pictures,

Subject to perennial scan with specific intent,

To lock on to a single mutilated frame,

Yet the content in vivid colours displaying,

Deeply etched with exhilarated emotions,

Mind's retaining folds shoring in abundance,

The paints of sorrow, joy, pain and relief,

Unlike the woven canvas of traditional art,

A medium of slow and prolonged decay,

These pictures of memory quickly dissolve,

Without the holding frame of experience,

A retaining anchor of the image set adrift,

In the vast sea of fathomless consciousness,

Deep felt within the ramparts of emotions,

A solid mooring assigned of superior strength,

Withstanding the vagaries of inhibiting stress,

These ageless treasures of the distant past,

Are my companion in my life's lonely hours,

Life rich in experience of relations fostered,

Empowering love lavishly given and received,

From a mind of pure intent to a creation,

So endowed with beauty and grandeur supreme,

As I close my eyes in deep slumber all frames fuse,

A single luminescent picture of divine splendour.

DELIVERANCE FROM THE UNKNOWN

An endless ocean murky and dark, low hanging mist,

All sense of dimension lost in a solitary world I exist,

Knowing not the path nor destination I mindless swim,

Gasping for breath, I rest my drained and aching limb,

Sinking to the bottom, I discover in breathing no strain,

Pure energy of translucent swirls penetrating my brain,

A kaleidoscope of complex images that no sense convey,

Multitude of contorted demons on my wretched self, prey,

Fear wells up in my heart and a throbbing rhythm ensue,

Ensnared like an animal my tortured mind seeks rescue,

I wake with a cold sweat from this multi-layered dream,

Transported out of the subliminal drowning in a stream,

From deeper levels of my awareness like a tide abated,

Obliterated through a mind that seeks logic unmitigated,

I savour the deliverance from the unconscious realm.

Gratitude for the wakefulness that my fears overwhelm.

I wake from sweating in a fevered dream,

Drenched with fears of the softly slaughtered day,

That gentle, dull, unrolling flow

Which runs as quickly as a rapid-running stream,

Or rushes like my panicked heartbeat may,

Or I am numb, as if its passing stuns.

Underneath our life, stranger meanings lie –

Strange link, strange logic, strange movement,

A second network grows and quietly gleams,

And when our lives our done, we will not die –

We will burn like life bestowing million suns.

DEMON OR DELIVERER?

Assembled multitude in finery and jocund attitude,

Grease paints a deception, the revellers vicissitude

A thousand Ramas in battlement with arrows arrayed,

Aim toward the ten headed Ravana mighty portrayed,

Setting sun in a symbolic journey the horizon descend,

Fiery missiles depart the taut strings in parabolic bend,

The roar ascends the heavens as the foe is brightly lit,

An arsenal deployed in an act, the very core to split,

The pounding giant's heart is rent asunder in a blaze,

Flames leap skyward covering the battlefield in haze.

As I depart, a muted witness to this annual festivity,

My heart is burdened and doused as the dying embers,

The mighty Ravana now stands a mere skeleton smoking,

Yet again to resurrect in renewed grandeur hate stroking,

This play of conquering evil through violence is endless,

As the world in silent witness is held ransom and clueless,

Better way to understand what begets evil in man's mind,

Born of collective karma seeking a healing saviour to find,

Evil is met by evil in a fine masquerade as a redeemer,

A cycle of destruction propagated by a demonic deliverer.

DISSOLVING DELUSIONS

On my mind's wall hang many a pictures,

Subject to perennial scan with specific intent,

To lock on to a single mutilated frame,

Yet the content in vivid colours displaying,

Deeply etched with exhilarated emotions,

Mind's retaining folds shoring in abundance,

The hue of sorrow, joy, pain and relief,

Unlike the woven canvas of traditional art,

A medium of slow and prolonged decay,

These pictures of memory quickly dissolve,

Without the holding frame of experience,

A retaining anchor of the image set adrift,

In the vast sea of fathomless consciousness,

Deep felt within the ramparts of emotions,

A solid mooring assigned of superior strength,

Withstanding the vagaries of inhibiting stress,

These ageless treasures of the distant past,

Are my companion in my life's lonely hours,

Life rich in experience of relations fostered,

Empowering love lavishly given and received,

From a mind of pure intent to a creation,

So endowed with beauty and grandeur supreme,

I close my eyes in deep meditation as all frames fuse,

A single luminescent picture of divine splendour.

DIVINE MERGER

To all celestial beings a subtle denial,

An apparition so potent in radiance,

Your presence in me a state surreal,

Moment of elation of unbound variance,

Unlike the fading rainbow in summer rain,

Indelible your hues in my being remain.

As the multi-forked bolt the nimbus tears,

Your vastness my thirsting essence rents,

A merger through a fusing heat that sears,

An amalgamation devoid of duality of intents,

All elements transformed in this new creation,

I stand transformed bereft of differentiation.

NEEM FLOWERS

The sweet scented fragrance in the breeze gently wafted,

Intoxicating mix with the moist air for a new task drafted,

Caressing my being drenching me in a lovely embrace,

My senses sought its very font in the dense verdant space,

Seeking the cause of these outpouring vapours to relish,

Close at hand, greedy for satisfaction a constant replenish,

Amplifying the gentle air infused with an inherent force,

My eyes beheld a cluster of tiny white blossoms dancing,

In the perfumed wind, a rocking, a delightful prancing,

Like stars twinkling in the sky on cloudless dark night,

Terrestrial galaxy delights my very senses in a new light.

DREAM WORLD

Waves upon waves crash upon the mind's shore,

In a vessel of indiscernible nature I am set adrift,

Pulled by a force beyond nature in a mythical lore,

An ocean enveloped in thick fog of constant shift,

A turmoil that blanks out the perception of space,

Destination unknown and bearing of no consequence,

Melded to the very elements, self exists sans a trace,

Yet I am aware of an identity, a unique semblance.

To aid no astral reference nor a functioning compass,

A travel, eternal, in all dimensions of space and time,

This domain, a strange landscape of instant trespass,

A kaleidoscope of time flows with no logic or rhythm,

In this enfolded space brief, potent memories reside,

Imprinted in lives gone bye thru a matrix indelible,

Decoded into being by a manifesting concomitant tide,

Resurrecting images and conveys messages impeccable.

Archetypes dance; the Trickster, the Mother and more,

Yet serenely laid out in my cocooned chamber inviolate,

I am the spectator and the artist in this theatrical lore,

Duality of perception emerging for a gist to precipitate,

Unknowing to the awareness my ambience transform,

A subtle change cast in this ocean of thoughts surging,

Billion, billion strokes of inerasable intent, a cuneiform,

A Karmic code of infinite complexity, perennial evolving.

EMERALD VORTEX

Dark clouds hang motionless in anticipation imminent,

Awaiting a signal, the accumulated moisture to discharge,

Code, deciphered by Arctic winds and the warm current,

The winds clear in a hurry, guided by the countless gorge,

Dispel the expectant rain to bare a sky, a morphing mask,

Making my descent into the valley a less ominous task,

Hills are alive with chirping birds and butterflies prance,

Flowers of many hue in fading glory at the summer's end,

Shivering blades of grass with clinging dew drops dance,

A melody nature imparts, in a complex motion portend,

Twisting blade flexes its green sinew, in its magnificence,

A song is in my heart, as I drink deep nature's brilliance.

Contour of the land, the verdant valleys deeply sketched,

Gently soaring peaks of varying heights, silhouetted relief,

Sudden thrust of land atop the hill, a crown etched,

An afterthought in the tectonic process, an impulse brief,

Unrestrained magma stress locked by the unyielding crust,

Failed volcanic vent shut by this superheated rocky thrust.

I give wings to my thoughts and soar above the landscape,

Patterns in some mathematical progression unknown yet,

Etched by glacial torrent and icy winds, undulating shape,

Ordained through a causal flow of forces in sequence set,

Emerald vortex shimmers in rhythmic pattern as the Sun,

A perpetual witness to the superb work nature spun.

FESTIVAL PRAYER

Sky lit up with the radiant red splash of fireworks,

Is but the vision of the splattered blood of the innocents,

When I see the hissing sparklers, throwing dying embers,

A sight of carnage of the Dalits in their blazing dwellings,

Sound of crackers exploding in rapid incessant sequence,

I hear the stuttering gun fire in the crowded market place,

Like the darkness that falls as the festive lamps are put out,

My heart sinks in desperation a perennial remedy to find,

How can I celebrate this beautiful festival of light?

Joyful tribute of conquest of evil by truth and knowledge,

Pray for an avatar Oh! Narasimha, your talons sharpened,

Destroy, dispel the darkness of untruth and blinding ego,

The Vedas, Upanishads and Gita, to the world we gave,

In its essence, many holy ones world religions established,

May again be governed by sages, a nation standing proud,

A beacon to the world, establishing a path of eternal truth.

FLIGHT OF THE ARROW

An adept warrior on a fast charcoal steed,

Elegantly poised, erect as a marble column,

Bow in hand, eye intense focused on a deed,

Landscape adorns this image, a class solemn,

Rider and stallion well trained a rare breed,

On a loyal mission or task, close to his bosom.

The bow aligned perfect a mental reflection,

Arrow at an impeccable point on the string,

Tension straining each fibre twisted to perfection,

Mind focused on the target, a stillness to bring,

Flawless union, archer and goal an intersection

Body and mind, a fused tool to release the string.

The arrow travels, life gained, with sure intent,

Archer rides, his very being on the missile impart,

Perfect focus all elements to unite and augment,

Target to seek, perfect impact, a masterly art,

By supernal power the target into his being orient,

The flight of the arrow culminates ere it depart.

GIFT FROM THE COSMIC ARCHITECT

I tread along this weary path aching bones complain,

My taut knuckles white against the cold of my winter,

A journey coursing through the travails of life plain,

Burdened mind seeking rest from turmoil and splinter,

Worn thin through constant usage my exterior wares,

A soiled garment trailing the soil in tatters and tares.

My eyes are sharply focused, a sight well bestowed,

Relentless search in every printed word a meaning,

To the purpose of life, this reality so void and hollowed,

Birth and death are but terminal stages in a gleaning,

The sower knows what crop or the quality of yield,

Through close knowledge of the seed and the lush field.

I closed my tired eyes and withdrew into my heart,

Praying to the cosmic architect for an end to the wrath,

Of knotted and knurled construct from my mind depart,

That very moment I opened my eyes and beheld a path,

There stood a child of wisdom, holding out a hand,

Guidance to a purpose I know not in this mysterious land.

She is given to me in this ripe age, perchance a reason,

Wisdom is her nature, a jewel reflecting the creation,

Unchanging yet evolving, a constant force in every season,

A pendent resting on my breast feeling my heart's elation,

This nurturing act stills my restless and turbulent mind,

The eternal calmness on your face, a new meaning I find.

IN YOUR EMBRACE

Lost in your vast and infinite expanse,

My solitude is oppressively exhibit,

A flotsam drifting on a vehicle of time,

Seemingly aimless and yet a purpose,

Deeply etched in your cosmic scheme,

A destination in my cyclic existence.

I long for association, knowing not,

Fuelled by every element far reaching,

Beyond the constraints of space time,

The apparent infinitude of manifest,

Is but the reflection of primal light,

Mirrored in this display of illusion

LONGING FOR LIGHT

In the labyrinth of my turbulent mind,

A perennial darkness hangs turgid,

I am the mind's eye searching to find,

Meaning in a composition so rigid.

My rational thoughts move incremental,

Losing the thread of connectivity,

This viscous flow in nature fundamental,

Disjointed vision lacking objectivity,

In this dark and meaningless feature,

The true self is embedded omniscient,

All knowing light of illumining nature,

Spark lit by cessation of flow incessant

MOMENTS OF PERCH

Seeking riches I take flight between resident chores,

Tarry a while to savour the sweet concoction and taste,

Intellectual nectar and fruit as darting glance explores,

A refuge where a luscious past to be reviewed in haste,

Regurgitated to a heady mix enriched in leisurely chew,

To distil to its full potency, a new knowledge as residue.

In these moments of perch, a jaunt through the past,

Evokes nuggets of wisdom filtered in a sieving lattice,

Therein resting eager for the rolling dice recurrent cast,

Needy choice in a new pattern for retention or release,

A tapestry of interwoven images in my synaptic frame,

Knowledge generation is the current name of the game.

The tempest of life tosses me in this ocean turbulent,

Instinct for survival holds on to the ropes of human ties,

Tattered and worn are these by constant usage virulent,

Only hopes are shattered planks bereft of sustaining ties,

These timbers are the knowledge imprints that ferried,

My imperishable soul to the new shores divinely decreed.

MONTHLY LETTER OF A BENEFACTOR

My narration is unique, for strange are the ways,

In this world of human kind, a common veneer runs,

Deep in our consciousness like a subterranean river,

Unknown, unfathomed and dormant to waking moments,

A simple letter he wrote and a small sum to soothe a pain,

By poverty and destiny imposed upon this aging mother,

Pouring out his heart, a participation in spirit,

Collating his earthly experience, a consolation he offered,

Divine blessings much bestowed, he had been fortunate,

Blessed with good health, knowledge and decent wealth,

But of all these gifts, a gem, a desire to alleviate suffering,

Of his fellow brethren in some way his assets permit.

The parchment he wrote these embalming words,

Made by some village craftsman from collected waste,

Calligraphy of patterns interwoven of enriching thought,

Erases the tear and shines a ray of hope when in despair,

His words were not of the intellect to inspire discourse,

Prayer for pain alleviation and a sum for monthly upkeep,

So her son may pursue his studious ambition,

Seeking a career to care for her in her aging days,

This benefactor tireless kept this bond for many years,

Until his health and feeble hand the pen no more hold,

The last message from his hospital bed was brief,

The essence being all his work now rests with the divine.

A doctor came and stood by his side, of bewitching beauty,

They said she had an intellect rare and healing touch.

In a sweet voice she said 'How shall I call you?'

For I held you with affection every moment of my life.

Shall I call you Sir! But that would be too formal,

Shall I call you 'The Holy One' but I know you are humble,

So I shall call you my 'Grand Dad'

For to the lady to whom you were a monthly joy,

I am her granddaughter and my life to you I dedicate.

MUTUAL NOURISHMENT

I was a weakling sprout, breaking ground,

My tender stems and fledgling leaves found,

You standing tall, reaching for the heavens blue,

Me thought that I can find a friendship true.

Your girth was immeasurable with rough bark,

Your limbs spread out, a perch for the lark,

You protected me from the searing tropical heat,

That on your immense canopy relentless beat.

You were the mammoth standing in eerie silence,

Full of life and vigour, an existence of resilience,

My supple tentacles find solace in your embrace

Sustained and nourished, I now my future face.

Many years pass, now my sinew thick and strong,

Envelope your surface, a twisted journey prolong,

To the very lofty heights an existence integral,

I rejoice in your presence now deemed inseparable.

The nimbus in the sky thunders, the wild wind roars,

A surging energy creeps from the very roots soars,

To the last vestiges of the mighty oak in a reach,

To plunge the storm's fury in a flash and screech.

In an instant the mighty tree is split and scarred,

All its foliage and shielding bark perennial charred,

Shuddering, by some miracle, I cling to this drab pole,

With my energy, this lifeless form, I constantly console.

Many summers, my strength immense, I stand high,

Within my frame the once mighty tree lifeless lie,

My caresses ever stronger in gratitude to my existence,

Desire in some way, to provide a nourishing sustenance.

One spring morn, lo and behold, sprouts a tender shoot,

From this entombed carcass, dormant life finds root,

My joy knows no bounds, perhaps my hopes rewarded,

Enduring desire finds expression by a new life awarded.

MY TRUE NATURE

The green algae floating in rhythmic dance,
Caressing fog swirling above the murky waters,
A gentle tease for the flotsam to daintily prance,
Slender legged flies hop and skip the dross.
Thick layer of moss a heavy ornate coat,
Every timber boasts glistening in the morning dew,
Transmuted to the very elemental state I float,
The very nature my handy work perennial new.
An entity indescribable, distant to decaying matter,
Resting at will in every atom, vibrant and awake,
Manifestation is my ballet on the cosmic altar,
Perfect law unfolds in every form I undertake.
Transforming yet immutable and eternal my essence,
I reside in the nature of man in his trillion cells,
I am the beauty of the flower and its sweet fragrance,
I am the immeasurable force that within the star dwells.
This is my nature beyond concept of the fickle mind,
Shackles of time chains me not to the future or past,
Ever present I am the One, free of domain, you find,
In the core of all, the binding web divinely cast.

MYSTIC RIVER

Flowing serenely through the wooded vale,

I chanced upon you as I broke free,

From the thicket and bramble that impale,

This tortured body, a wanderer on this lea.

I have, in my sojourn, many a river seen,

But you have the exhilarating quality to convey,

As the dawn which from darkness light wean,

A lustrous texture reflecting your laminar way.

As a trickling spring, a subterranean source,

You began your life, an unhindered course,

Many rivulets supplementing this vast concourse,

Thundering in ever increasing flow; a mighty force.

Potency bestowed to invigorate or mutate,

Magic fodder to the grain nourishment brought,

Even the mighty land and Pharaoh you subjugate,

You are my life's inspiration, I earnestly sought.

ON THE LAP OF SOPHIA

In comfort, I do not see the sustaining, reassuring hold,

My tiny hand rests upon your transforming, scripting arm,

Your wisdom like the heavenly cloak its caresses unfold,

My naked ignorance enfolded in your intelligent charm,

I look upon thine immaculate countenance shining bright,

Your cosmic form, the crown in mystic suspension adorn,

Held aloft by the winged cherubs unseen in human light,

Warping portal routing infinite wisdom celestial born.

Mother of wisdom, the primal cause and creative force,

Burn away the encrusted layers impeding nourishing feed,

Cast upon my throbbing soul through corrupting source,

Perceptions incrementally aggregated by sensory feed.

In the lap of Sophia, my Divine mother and teacher,

I shall remain your child seeking empowering wisdom,

State of perennial gratefulness from this mortal creature,

In the numerous existence until united in your kingdom.

PARTAKING

I stood like a tall cedar of Lebanon in this grove,

My roots running deep, a subterranean field,

Seeking the living waters you so abundantly gave,

A blessed life with many a harvest and copious yield.

Many a time I heard your call, an enticing respite,

I lingered on this shore savouring nectar sweet,

Bonds of love this frail frame did hold tight,

Stroking the last embers an absent blaze to induce.

Your fragrance intoxicating I did inhale deep,

In this very act my earthly breathe abated,

I took wings to your bosom in eternal sleep,

Ferried for a purpose my earthly mind discern not.

Four score and dozen years you rested in my being,

Copious blessing bestowed through me to one and all,

An infinitesimal chalice of your creation, ever flowing,

Now it rests in your divine hand for a purpose to enthral.

POPPY FIELDS

A century passed since the million valiant fell,

A generation gone consigned to fading past,

No soul remain the deeds of courage to tell,

Yet they remain etched in nature's canvas vast,

Every drop of blood that was shed, a holy breath,

Sprouting in glory, swaying in the wintry draught,

The dark centre a symbol of culminating death,

Benevolent bestowed to end the agony fraught.

As the font of blood on rupture of the flesh tender,

Ruddy petals, token of war's perennial tribulation,

The quartered lobes, a shape so delicately slender,

A symbol of the cycle of decay and regeneration.

This flower is a symbol of peace and resurrection,

A hope for mankind lost in the slumber of insolence,

Intent on selfish gain and profit through insurrection,

Behold nature's gift of the human soul in transference.

Man has not learned from pain of incessant conflict,

From the poppy fields of Flanders, the cold terrain,

To poppy fields of Afghan more grievous pain to inflict,

A market place of armaments deployed with no restrain.

Violence breeds violence, a proven trap of no escape,

Assuage the frayed emotions with the spiritual balm,

We are on a short journey in this cosmic landscape,

An ordered domain of unfathomable, perennial calm.

PRAYER AT DAWN

Darkness dispelling dawn breaks over the vast ocean,

Surging currents of hope every beam of light brings,

To weed out the dying foliage, its purpose served,

Your life giving energy coaxes the hesitant bud open,

Bursting petals to invite the nectar seeking swarm,

Caress my withering body, invigorate my aching soul.

As I lift my eyes to you in sublime veneration,

Bestow upon me the wisdom to surrender and accept,

The revelations that every unfolding moment brings,

As your rising heat stirs the sea to spawn life giving dew,

The parched land gratefully receives through every pore,

So too reveal the higher purpose of my life in your grace.

PRAYER OF DEDICATION

To you my creator and sustainer I genuflect in gratitude,

From one in ten thousand you chose me as your disciple,

Poured your primeval energy in to my being in plenitude,

Resulting wisdom, your gift is my elemental principle,

For a life these years of love to be in a mission relentless,

To elevate your every creation to their potential limitless.

Not worthy, this human frame, slave to temptation,

Nourish me through your eternal and sustaining presence,

Knowing every element in my body is a reverberation,

Of timeless beauty of pure radiance, your infinite essence,

Till the day you claim me to your loving bosom,

Grant me the delight to toil in making every soul blossom.

REFLECTION & REQUIEM

I sat among the tombs enmeshed by thriving weed,

Reading inscriptions, struggling to kindly unfold,

Many years or short life of mentionable deed,

Earthly image now cast in an innocuous mound,

Perhaps a chance fodder for a fortunate seed,

Inculcating decaying matter into a vegetative fold.

A thousand memories floods my weary mind,

Encouraging words whispered, a path to learn,

Strong hands in need my hesitant steps to find,

Hardships, pain endured a decent living to earn,

Frugal in your needs yet lavishing love and kind,

Made me strong and my spirit, a creative urn.

In a silence potent with meaning from this tomb,

Your voice ever echoes in every crevice of my heart,

Tutored well through tacit stroking in the womb,

Constant presence in every need an indelible part,

Nurtured me to take flight, greater pastures to roam,

Now I rest my thoughts on these stones ere I depart.

A prayer of gratitude from my still lips emanate,

To the living you have given with values affluent,

In the knowledge that this is but an isolation innate,

Spirit empowering potion my integral constituent,

Your image I carry in every act, an elevated state,

Where all-purpose towards a singularity congruent.

JOURNEY IN THE VALLEY

Verdant plains roll by my window,

As my car in steady, efficient hum,

Consumes the freshly laid Tarmac,

Hurried chore to reach a destination,

Beyond the rushing arching trees,

A canopy nature wove in many years.

Distant rolling hills on both sides,

Veiled by the moisture of rising heat,

Shimmers like a silken veil draped,

Around the countenance of a bride,

Hiding the beauty in million elements,

That collated these vast ramparts.

Distances, an illusion, only revealed,

By subtle differences of prominence,

Of each structure of tectonic fold,

Eons of patient incremental making,

A dedication to the cosmic artisan,

Omnipotent ever changing yet still.

REFLECTION ON A BEACH

The rocky coastline twists and turns,

White sands in the mid-day sun burns,

Hurrying crabs to the water's edge runs,

Crashing waves resonates of metallic urns.

This beat and rhythm, a melody enchanting,

Cool spray of salt upon my face depositing,

Baked dry by the merciless sun beating,

Upon every exposed terrain, incessant heating.

Between the heat and the cold life borders,

A survival and nourishment that nature orders,

Though life may appear in chaos and tatters,

There is a fine balance that ultimately matters.

LONGING FOR LIGHT

In the labyrinth of my turbulent mind,

A perennial darkness hangs turgid,

I am the mind's eye searching to find,

Meaning in a composition so rigid.

My rational thoughts move incremental,

Loosing the thread of connectivity,

This viscous flow in nature fundamental,

Disjointed vision lacking objectivity.

In this dark and meaningless feature,

The true self is embedded omniscient,

All knowing light of illumining nature,

Spark lit by cessation of flow incessant.

SEEKING THE ORIGIN

From the moss encrusted abode, my icy dungeon,

I exit the one creaking door that held me captive,

A burdensome chore lifting the heavy metal latch,

To a gloomy terrain of alien hue and distorted contour,

The rolling fog by some mysterious and devious design,

Hangs low, creating an image of a personal cocoon,

As I tread the ground, an intimate connection lost,

An ethereal feel of floating buoyed and directed,

By my thoughts which distort like the swirling eddies,

Leaving a wake of perturbation in this dynamic field.

The caressing of my senses through sweet scented breath,

The cacophony of the never ceasing justifying thoughts,

The tingling touch of the illusion with a quality of a lover,

Deter my progress and induce an oblivious stupor,

A comfort zone dulling my mind in a temporal domain,

I pull away from the numbed feel wishing for revelation,

Of the intended path guiding my steps in this darkness,

Night persists no illuminating ray ever pierces this space,

Deflected by the swelling ignorance of the logical mind,

Many a birth and death pass as my soul labours on.

Utterly my ego deflated I fall to the ground in prostration,

The reality then is revealed as I make intimate contact,

With the ground of being, the Divine light that illumines,

Shines not from the cosmos but at in state of total void,

Beyond the savouring senses and the roving restless mind,

A billion sparks of miniscule dimension hidden deep,

Penetrates my being and every pore in my body,

I see the shores of the ocean of pure light within,

Now I know the source from which I came and

To which eternal I will return.

SINGULARITY - BEGINNING AND END

Silver bow arches and sparkles in the darkened firmament,

Million stars in dazzling and radiant celestial display,

Fiery cauldron in harmony dance, a circular movement,

Churning the cosmic ocean, a vortex in glistening array.

The distant hills silhouetted in the dusk, undulating mass,

Shaped by the winds a sleepy giant on the water's edge lay,

Breaking the surf and the immense waves lest it trespass,

Green meadow and the grazing sheep in the sheltered bay.

Lone lighthouse stands on the hill, a silent inert sentinel,

Like a telescope in an heavenward extra-terrestrial scan,

Shaft of light beam sweeps over the rumbling death knell,

Guide to ancient Maori mariners in a homeward sojourn.

I gaze upon the starry realm from this earthly company,

A rug of jewels, the shining of fusion heat contained taut,

Mysterious energy, conductor of this cosmic symphony,

Forms in many dimensions, an image of supreme thought.

I who perceive this vision may mind be unshackled,

From the turmoil of false perception of my senses lend,

May my spirit sore past this limiting temporal tabernacle,

Quest for its source, in singularity of beginning and end.

SUBTLE LANGUAGE OF NATURE

In the intricate pattern and feel of the rose petal,

The translucent design in the wings of the dragonfly,

Shaped by eons by incremental change to finer mettle,

Nature's code and causal laws mind's probing defy.

Shapes to read in an ever changing nomadic cloud,

Myriad sketch autumn leaves cast on the forest floor,

Shaped by the tortuous air, like a sweeping shroud,

Worn by an roving mendicant, the fine earth scour.

Humming of the honeybee seeking delectable nectar,

Harmonious chirping of the crickets in the evenfall,

Balmy rhythm to quell, a divinely ordained benefactor,

An ensemble and orchestration, a gift at nature's call.

I close my eyes to behold your countenance so fair,

Radiance of a thousand suns your perennial feature,

A form perceived through insightful meditative fare,

Million steps through the subtle language of nature,

This journey of ascension to the very core I seek,

In slow mutation, I now nature's subtle language speak.

SUSTENANCE

The sweltering heat shimmers on the land,

With patience the furrows dug, planted seed,

Exposed, covered with soil by loving hand,

Nurtured by the breaking sweat, a hesitant bead,

Suspended on the brow, little rivulets run slow,

Descends from facial crevice to the land below.

Mornings cool as the drifting fog from the sea,

Vital moisture stripped of salt by the torrid heat,

Finds an abode in the foliage of the thorny tree,

Droplets bejewelled in a sunlight capturing feat,

A day's fluid for the desert insect vital need,

Precious sustenance through nature's loving feed.

I cross the stormy sea, my sails in the tempest torn,

Tossed and battered in the frothy eddy of turmoil,

Aching limbs and stretched sinew a frame well worn,

Reduced by constant endeavour in an unending toil,

Seek a moment relief, a calm and undulating motion,

A respite and droplets of dew, a rejuvenating potion.

As the storm clouds break in the dark and dreary night,

Sirius, the lone star, shines bright with ominous lore,

You were to the ancient Polynesians a guiding light,

You are my shining hope to reach the comforting shore.

I follow your incorruptible path stationed far above,

To the very land where awaits my joy and eternal love.

THOUGHTS ON THE ICY MOUND

Fresh crystals packed into a high mound,

White hillock of layered flakes fractals thin,

Shaped by playful hands into missiles round,

Hurled in frolic with gay abandon pure within,

The darting feet and laughter in the chill air,

Many a cloud from the inner warmth an icy rest,

Many little feet knead the snow in a path fair,

Ascending I look with longing upon the crest,

I sit down watching as fresh snow in a slow drift,

From a sky tinged grey as the hue of the land,

My view aspiring an elevated mood, attempted lift,

The dampened spirit, to greener times at hand,

A spring of flowers and smells, a radical shift,

Two sides of all existence, the opposing poles,

So vital in our lives, the darkness and the light,

Waxing and waning energy in creative roles,

Immense is your expression revealing your might.

TO MY SPIRITUAL COMPANION

A thousand thoughts, varied in content unread,

The empty chairs, fresh linen and unslept bed,

You were in the midst of my life, strong presence,

Indelible marks of your diverse permeating essence,

In all that you touched, a million lives to comfort,

A tireless mandarin, outpouring immense effort,

In healing and assuaging distressed, distraught minds,

You were the comforting domain, an oasis one finds,

Among the parched landscape and constricted space,

Liberating portal, a door to the uplifting grace,

Freeing minds, you surpassed the artificial ramparts,

Of religion, caste, narrow divides that duality imparts,

You resided in the oneness of love of all creation,

You sought the wisdom of the scribes and ancients,

Your aching soul sought the deep truth in science,

Your consciousness has transcended to a dimension,

Far beyond my reach, rudderless I float in this ocean,

Be my guiding star and companion in this cosmic sojourn,

To evolve beyond this relentless cycle of return.

THROUGH HIGHER REALM

Wafting in the breeze intoxicating yet imperceptible,

Propulsion of a jellyfish arrayed with shimmering tentacle,

A flotilla of gentile life forms, a consciousness receptacle,

Path determined by some distant destiny with no obstacle,

Softly rests on my meditating mind with some intuition,

Message to communicate of higher purpose in evolution,

Interlacing field of subtle information infusing every form,

Translation mirrored in resonance in this surging swarm,

My thoughts vibrate the very medium in a reflected wave,

In this radiant paradise I am an awestruck slave,

Process of life augmented by a symbiotic relation so rare,

Changing patterns and nature's tapestry a meaningful fare.

The very terrain I rest seems alive with muffled vibration

Of energy surging through my every sinew in celebration,

Culminating in my heart to evoke a tsunami of potency,

A resurrecting wisdom conveyed of higher competency,

I travel the higher realms of existence this very moment,

Knowing this lasts a brief span, this blissful movement.

VOICES OVER THE SURF

I sat amidst the spray from the breaking surf,

Transformed my inner being to an ethereal turf,

A power bestowed heightened senses to discern,

A kaleidoscope of voices thrown up from an urn,

Like ashes of the departed sown in the balmy wind,

To nature returned a temporal home this cycle find

In the distance, the mighty whale leads his pack,

Homing instinct this path and journey surely track,

This annual sojourn coded through million years,

Shoreward wind carries the clarion call all prey fears,

Symphony of a hundred notes his presence intimate,

This purpose a command or a love song to his mate.

On this sea I hear the deafening roar of ammunition,

A galley of war in the fog a ghostly definition,

Sails unfurled, the wind whistling, rigging taut,

Hundred hands loading the cannons victory sought,

An eerie mix of wounded cry and suppressed pain,

Chills my heart and a shiver runs down my spine.

Rudely waken from my dream on the water's edge,

Salty spray rests on my face as the dew on the hedge,

Perhaps an echo of my heart's cry, I hear a distant call,

Your holy presence by my side this summer evenfall,

Voices over the surf a concoction of emotion evoke,

But my heart this instant your eternal company invoke.

WEB OF DELIGHT

Silver thread glistening in the dawning light,

Subtle vibrations, a pulsing in the breeze mild,

To the discerning beholder, a veritable delight,

I am a lone spectator in this amphitheatre wild.

Fractured fragments of the secreted strand,

Dance like the hairs of Medusa, class serpentine,

Work in progress tarried a while for some errand,

With bated breath I see how the prey you confine.

You hold steady your senses alert feeling the air,

An approaching prey's beating wings does incite,

The web pulsates in response, a signal in your lair,

Imperceptible the trap laid yet a marvel in my sight.

You await still for the clueless wandering moth,

Heavy impact the net stretches, a vortex drawn,

Like the thirst seemingly quenched by the froth,

False sense of rest alleged ere the final end dawn.

My soul aches for this restful flight, a journey long,

Tired wings in endless search for its true abode,

Cast your net, a sweet trap, and do not prolong,

Rest in your sweet embrace and your spirit behold.

WHITE WATERS

Waters gurgling in gentle murmur upon which I stumble,

Million drops shriek descending the hillock green,

Over the boulders, polished pebbles and thorny bramble,

Dodging every corner and crevice to a destiny unseen,

Subject to nature's course, in a constant aberration,

Freeing the trapped air, the bubbles in uneven explosion,

Coordinated dancing, swirling waves in dynamic gyration,

A ballet, though chaotic in nature, an awesome exposition.

Strong breeze gliding over the frothy waters in motion,

Sweep up the rainbow hued spray in embrace of rapture,

Every moment is a shifting act and screaming commotion,

Vortices and eddies, the drifting flotsam formless rupture,

Swaying reed on the water's edge dance like the ballerina,

Flapping in the tumultuous flow in constant undulation,

Harmonious ovation of audience seated around the arena,

I too stand in awe, this sojourn of wondrous revelation.

TO MY DIVINITY

In every beat of my longing heart,

You are the force, the indelible part,

Each filament of my pulsing sinew,

You are the nourishing spirit that renew,

The vigour for life, an unabated desire,

To consummate a union, in an intense fire,

Transformed my elements into a force,

To redefine my earthly journey and course,

Into a transmuted substance made sublime,

Hence in my mind a presence beyond time,

Never waning in its intended purpose,

In you my being ever finds quieting repose.

CRY OF A TORTURED SOUL

It is with shuddering trepidation that I watch,

My perplexing dreams unfold on a canvas vast,

Every act, a subconscious element match,

Extricated in fine mettle and finely cast,

A multihued art upon a tapestry so delicate,

A painting of fine strokes and pattern intricate.

Distorted field of projection beyond time,

A perception of landscape defying logic,

A region of intricacy and quality sublime,

Past and future seem to merge by some magic,

There is only a vivid moment in my memory,

All reality twisted by some internal treachery.

All elements seem to defy every natural law,

Association and existence perfectly unbound,

Immense power within to counter every flaw,

Unharmed in this sojourn a new life found,

I ride the surging waves of towering magnitude,

I shame the wind to rise to great altitude.

Am I playing God or a mortal so bestowed,

Immense power and inherent capacity to change,

Reality but an element with fluidity endowed,

Extricated at my will in a subconscious exchange,

Blurring interface between the real and the fake,

Itself a test for some intuitive meaning to make.

Fluidity is the innate and all-pervading element,

Seeping in every crevice in this world to flaunt,

A creeping act to seek a buried essence rudiment,

To spin a yarn and my waking moments haunt,

A vast repository of my subliminal imprints in store,

Is the rich content for the apparent meaningless lore.

Oh! Tortured soul gasping for an identity true,

Escape from the darkened alleys damp with fear,

Desire for the warmth of sunshine and skies blue,

Give me wings of Cherubim to your presence near,

Prompting a path to elevate my consciousness anew,

The blessing of wisdom bestowed on the chosen few.